LOOK CLOSER

Visual Thinking Skills & Activities

by Nancy L. Johnson

Pieces of Learning

Cover design by Pat Bleidorn
Layout & Design by Stan Balsamo

©1996 Pieces of Learning
1990 Market Road
Marion IL 62959
polmarion@midamer.net
www.piecesoflearning.com

CLC0182
ISBN 1-880505-10-X
Printing No. 1098765
Printed in the U.S.A.

"The purpose of a book should be to trap the mind into doing its own thinking."

Christopher Morley

Dedication

To my bud, SAM
Extraordinary Feline and All Around Super Cat
who LOOKS CLOSER at all things great and small in a world
beset with humans who just don't SEE!

Acknowledgements

Thank you to all the talented artists who contributed
the illustrations: Joe Wayman, Katie Snell, Bill Jensen,
Greg Lawhun and Barbara Yonan.
A special thanks to Pat Bleidorn for illustrations
and cover design. As always, my love and appreciation to
Stan and Kathy Balsamo for layouts, graphic design and editing.

Introduction

To my friends it's known as The Great Near Disaster. I'm not sure exactly why it happens, but somehow, every now and then we human beings just know it's time to....WALLPAPER! Before we know it there is a stack of pattern books in front of our noses waiting for THE GREAT DECISION!

I will never forget the look on the saleswoman's face when she said, "Are you REALLY sure you want THAT pattern for your bathroom? Do you REALLY want those HUGE flowers to cover ALL the walls? Please try to visualize what HUNDREDS of bright RED poppies will look like every morning at 6 A.M. Do you have a husband or mother-in-law you're trying to get rid of, or what?"

But golly gee, they looked so pretty in the pattern book!

No, I really couldn't "see" what my bathroom would look like covered in poppies. Visualizing complete patterns has never been my forte. Thank goodness the saleswoman talked me out of it. Thank goodness I became an education consultant and not an interior decorator!

There are lots of us out there—people with poor visual skills; lazy learners who are stuck in traditional verbal, logical and sequential patterns of thinking. We are such good talkers—even though language can actually be a limiting factor in some communication and problem solving situations.

Powerful visual thinking skills lay trapped in the brain; skills just waiting to be set free and used to improve learning, life and the selection of appropriate wallpaper!

It's a challenge to think visually. But with a little patience, practice and perseverance——it works! Visual thinking is an active not passive process. Like a battery in a car, visual thinking jump starts the human brain and kicks it into a stronger, more flexible learning mode. Visual thinking is a must for all students including those with special needs. When combined with logical, abstract and creative thinking, visual thinking completes the process of critical thinking in the new classroom of the 21st century.

Hummm....Maybe just one wall of poppies and another wall of. . . .

What is Visual Thinking?

Trying to define thinking is a little like explaining how pigs fly. Interpret is probably a better word than define. Physiologists have their own specialized language that attempts to explain brain function while we educators have another. We do know that thinking takes place all the time, even when we sleep. The brain is always active, showing constant electrical activity. Thinking is both conscious and subconscious. However, most scientists agree that thinking would never happen if it was left totally up to the brain. A formula for thinking might look something like this:

MIND + BODY + NERVOUS SYSTEM + EMOTION = THINKING

Thinking can travel or be delivered along several paths:

WORDS (spoken or written language)

SYMBOLS (mathematical or scientific codes)

MENTAL PICTURES (imagination or images)

EMOTIONS (feelings, opinions or point of view)

KINESTHETIC (movement or motion)

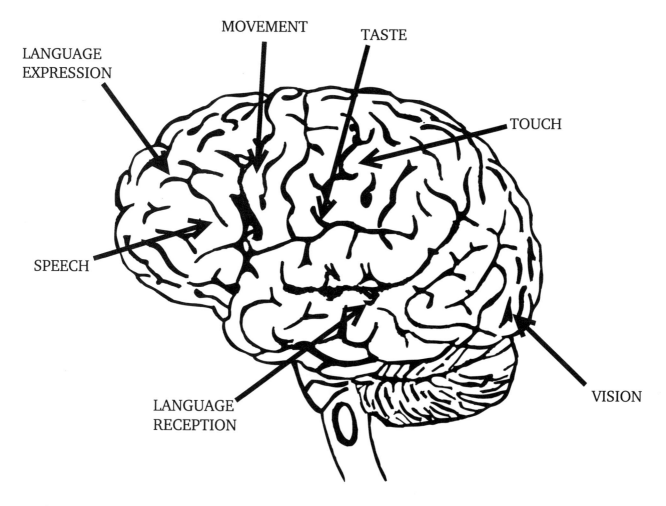

Visual Thinking Is ACTIVE Thinking

Visual thinking is a combination of two powerful mental operations: ANALYSIS and SYNTHESIS. Visual analysis happens when we look closer at something by dissecting it or breaking it into parts. Visual synthesis happens when we look closer at something by combining or bringing the parts together. The brain is going through a very ACTIVE process when it is thinking visually. Much, but not all of the activity occurs in the right hemisphere.

Visual thinking is a process by which we acquire and remember new information or retrieve old information by using our eyes. When new visual data enters the brain, it is transformed into electrical impulses discharged from the retina. The impulses then travel up the optic nerve into the cerebral cortex where they are stored as patterns between neurons. If the patterns are repeated several times, they are stored in our short term or long term memory. If they are not repeated, the visual thinking we have just done is quickly forgotten.

Visual thinking helps us understand or comprehend what we hear or read. As language enters the brain it is converted into images or visual patterns. The formula might look like this:

LANGUAGE + VISUAL THINKING = COMPREHENSION + UNDERSTANDING

Visual thinking also helps stimulate creative problem solving. As we see and draw mental pictures of the components of a problem the process of selecting the best solution becomes much more efficient and clear.

Who?

They're out there. The lucky ones; those humans with an innate, unusually dominant ability to think visually. Yes, we all use visual thinking in some way, but a few people are truly blessed. Their preferred learning style is visual or spatial. Just listen! They give themselves away with their descriptive language.

"LOOK at that!"
"SEE what I mean!"
"PICTURE this...."
"I can't VISUALIZE that as a realistic solution."
"I just don't SEE your point of view."
"Let's LOOK at the big PICTURE."
"Let's take a quick GLANCE at our options."
"He's a SIGHT for sore eyes."
"I prefer a more global VIEW."
"We'll try it and then OBSERVE the consequences."
"I ENVISION a real easy solution to that."
"I'll wait and WATCH what happens."
"I can't IMAGINE that happening to me!"
"Could you DRAW me a PICTURE of your idea?"
"SEEING is believing!"

Visual or spatial learners may not be as verbal as their peers. When they do talk, their comments will be filled with visual language. Because they notice small visual details that others might miss, their comments may be misinterpreted as negative criticism. Visual learners sometimes need more visual cues in order to completely understand problems.

For Visual/Spatial Learners:

- **Seeing Really Is Believing**

- **Seeing Is Communicating**

- **Seeing Is Understanding**

- **Seeing Is Learning**

A Question of Gender

Are males more innately visual or spatial than females? (I said spatial not special!) Yes, in some ways they are. Males and females seem to use different parts of the brain to do the same thing. Males seem to be able to acclimate objects in space better than females. They "see" in 3-D. The next time you pass a video arcade, stop and check the ratio of males to females. There will always be more males. When a male looks closer at objects in a two-dimensional picture or drawing, he sees their exact shapes and components just as they really are. But when he looks closer at objects in a three-dimensional picture or drawing, he is able to visualize, see or imagine the objects in space. A male's keen **spatial perception skills** makes this all possible. It may also explain why there are more male architects and chess champions. Males also seem to have a better innate perception of north, south, east and west. But it's not perfect. When it fails, they hate to stop and ask someone else for directions!

We females may be able to communicate better both verbally and nonverbally, but when it comes to reading a road map or packing the trunk of the car, the guys have it over us hands down! However, females do have much better fine motor skills and **memory for detail**. It is called **proximal** or close-up vision. Pick up any newspaper, turn to the society column and read the wedding announcements. The bride's dress will always be described in detail! Females may get confused when trying to read a road map but they will never forget that there was a Pizza Hut with a gravel parking lot at the edge of town, a big white house with pillars, rose bushes and a swing set near the town square and a Shell station with only one working bathroom and a broken car wash across from the Dairy Queen.

The activities in this book are designed to help both male and female students improve their visual skills as well as enrich their knowledge and understanding of each other.

Are You Visually Illiterate?

Excuses!   Excuses!   Excuses!

"I don't need to teach that visual stuff. The art teacher does that!"

"Visual thinking is drawing pictures, isn't it? I hate drawing pictures."

"I don't have TIME to do visual thinking! Friday afternoons only happen once a week, ya know."

"Oh sure, the kids just love it. But what in the world does visual thinking have to do with REAL education?

"What if HE walks in while I'm teaching that crazy visual stuff? What if SHE walks in?"

The Great Surprise!

I had those blinders on again. You know the ones I mean. Those mind setting blinders that trap the brain into a straight and narrow thinking pattern. So easy. So safe, comfortable and secure.

I thought that the sole purpose of teaching visual thinking would be to stimulate flexibility in those left brained, sequential, logical thinking kids (and their teachers). I thought that was enough. A noble cause, with practical solutions. Once I discovered that my ideas and activities really worked I stopped looking for other possibilities or applications. I clamped those blinders on my brain nice and tight, never bothering to look left or right. Then it happened. While field testing some of the activities with teachers and their students, I discovered a whole new world of benefits and uses for visual thinking. Of course, the information was there all the time. But it took a bunch of kids and their observant teachers to get my attention. It all started with comments like these:

*"Miss Johnson, you know those visual thinking activities you demonstrated in my classroom last fall, the ones that were supposed to stimulate **flexible thinking**? Well, I don't know how much they helped my students' flexible thinking, but I've really noticed a difference in **attention spans**. My students seem more focused and able to pay attention longer."*

*"When I use the overhead projector to do the visual **problem solving** my students' eyes seem to be glued to the screen. It is so quiet in my classroom, you can hear a pin drop. It's tuff for them to talk and think at the same time. This stuff is great for a group of kids who are non stop talkers! They really are becoming **better listeners**."*

*"It's a miracle! Finally I have something that really helps students who suffer from **attention deficit**. Visual thinking seems to be the missing piece in the learning puzzle for them."*

*"You've done it to me again, Nancy Johnson! You and your visual thinking have forced me to change my teaching methods again. The lessons are driving my gifted kids crazy. It's wonderful! I know the **challenge** is really good for them."*

*"Nan, just a short note about your visual problem solving activities. Did you know that they help improve **memory**? I use a visual activity as **readiness** before teaching an important concept or skill. It seems to get the brain ready for learning. I also use a visual activity at the end of the same lesson. That seems to help the brain retain the information I've just taught. And, the best news of all: My students really **enjoy** doing the activities. They are quick to remind me if I forget the 'seeing stuff'. It's definitely becoming habit forming. Thanks!"*

*"The students in my resource room bug me every day to do more of the visual puzzles. I really think it's helped improve their attitudes about school and learning. It's been a long time since some of my students have had such **success** in school."*

The key words collected from the teachers' comments are more than enough reasons for adding more visual thinking to the curriculum.

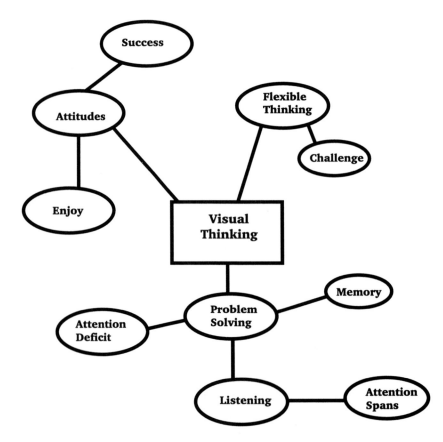

Well, there it goes again. Did you hear it? That funny ripping, splitting noise? It's those mind-setting blinders being torn from my head——again!

Visual Thinking

MUST BE

encouraged,

taught,

stimulated,

aroused, cultivated,

inspired, developed,

exercised, activated,

improved, expanded,

assimilated, utilized,

learned and

ENJOYED!

Why?

As some readers thumb through the pages of this book their first thoughts may be those of confusion or mystery. After all, why should teachers and parents be concerned about a student's visual thinking abilities? Don't teachers have enough to do? Why should visual thinking be an automatic consideration in curriculum development? Isn't it just a bunch of fun and games? Don't most parents think their children get enough visual stimulation by watching television? Isn't poor visualization just a matter of getting kids fitted with the proper glasses? The **WHY?** can be explained in five reassuring ways.

1. SPATIAL INTELLIGENCE: Thomas Armstrong in his book **Multiple Intelligences in the Classroom** (ASCD 1994) does an excellent job in explaining Gardner's Theory of Multiple Intelligences. Most humans will be highly intelligent in one of seven different ways: Logical/Mathematical, Linguistic, Intrapersonal, Interpersonal, Spatial, Musical, and Bodily/Kinesthetic. Spatial Intelligence includes several powerful visual skills that will help children do 'good life' as well as 'good school'. Armstrong lists several key materials and methods that exemplify and stimulate this particular intelligence. Some examples: visual thinking exercises, computer graphics software, mind-maps and graphic organizers, visual pattern seeking, visual puzzles and mazes, optical illusions, visual awareness activities, picture literacy and idea sketching. Although strong Spatial Intelligence seems to be innate in **some** children, it can be stimulated and improved in **all** children.

2. FUTURE JOBS AND CAREERS: Many economists and sociologists are predicting that by the time today's children reach middle age they will have changed jobs a minimum of ten times and careers three times. Over 50 per cent of those 10 jobs and three careers will require some level of visual problem solving. Seventy per cent will require computer literacy. Strong, confident visual thinking will facilitate frequent shifts in employment. Let's face it! It will mean more money in higher wages, promotions, and bonuses. The competitive job market of the 21st Century will reward those who are prepared with sharp, rapid visual problem solving skills.

3. STUDY SKILLS/ TEST TAKING: Doing 'good school' still means good study skills and good grades. However many teachers now use graphic organizers for student portfolios; students must learn how to brainstorm and outline in less traditional ways. Thinking visually is also a mandate for today's age of computer technology. Homework today might be a mindMap on a computer screen. Most standardized achievement tests as well as I.Q. tests incorporate visual reasoning and recall. Remember this question?

Which Shape is congruent?

Most importantly, good study skills and test taking skills build self confidence which leads to a more positive self esteem.

4. 'AT RISK' STUDENTS: These days in education it's alphabet soup. From LD (Learning Disability), BD (Behavior Disability), ADD (Attention Deficit Disorder) to ADHD (Attention Deficit/Hyperactivity Disorder) the labels keep coming. What's a parent to do? What's a teacher to do? When 'At Risk' students are fed a steady, daily diet of visual thinking they reap the benefits of better reasoning ability, better concentration, better listening ability, longer attention span and clearer short term and long term memory. Some 'At Risk' students experience the real joy of learning for the first time because their teachers or parents empower them with visual problem solving techniques. When students begin to look at common things in uncommon ways their imaginations flourish. Memory of facts and specific details improves. Good memory improves study habits and test taking skills. Just imagine what that does for a student's self esteem!

5. GIFTED AND TALENTED STUDENTS: Some G/T students insulate themselves from intellectual risk taking. They become experts at coming up with the right answer because in most classrooms that is the kind of thinking that is rewarded with good grades. They are conditioned to be inflexible thinkers, lacking an appreciation for different opinions. That will surely get them into trouble in the 21st century with those expected ten jobs and three careers. Visual thinking activities empower G/T students to use more than logical/sequential thinking while at the same time improve their tolerance for frustration and failure. Visual creativity stimulates the gifted brain to think in new patterns, seeing different points of view. Gifted students will experience a heightened awareness of people, emotions and the environment.

Note: Share a copy of the previous five points with administrators and/or parents. Communication and accountability are important. Let the "powers that be" know the reasons for including visual thinking in the regular curriculum.

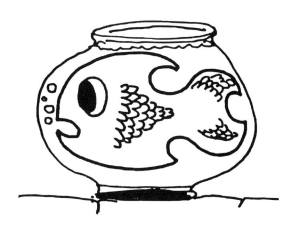

When?

It's Everywhere! It's Everywhere!

So, who needs good visual thinking skills?

YOU DO, if there is.....

...a closet to organize.

...a basketball play to diagram.

...a suit or dress to design.

...an astronomy quiz to pass.

...a carpenters floor plan to read.

...a road map to follow.

...an achievement test to take.

...a head of hair to style.

...a photograph to appreciate.

...a bouquet of flowers to arrange.

...a sign language speech to deliver.

...a traffic symbol to obey.

...a sculpture to enjoy.

...a puzzle to complete.

...another person's body language to interpret.

...a farmer's field to plan.

...a film to watch.

...a graph to analyze.

...a soccer game to win.

...a picture to draw.

...a wardrobe to coordinate.

...a house to build.

...a sale to advertise.

...a computer to program.

...an electrical circuit to wire.

...a chess game to win.

...a musical score to write.

...a wild animal to track.

...a sports car to detail.

...a blueprint to read.

...an accident to describe.

...a birthday cake to decorate.

...an art gallery to manage.

...a comic strip to draw.

...a video to shoot.

...a rebus story to explain.

...a pamphlet to design and layout.

...a mural to complete.

...a diary to illustrate.

...a scrapbook to organize.

...a quilt to design.

...a mind map due for your portfolio.

...an origami project in art.

...an engine to take apart, repair, and put back together.

...a floor exercise in gymnastics to choreograph.

...a crime to report.

...a poster to complete using calligraphy.

...a wallpaper pattern to choose!

Look Closer At The CAREERS That Require Visual Thinking:

Advertising: Graphic Designer, Art Director, Computer Layout Artist, Illustrator, Calligrapher, Window Dresser, Color Consultant, Photographer, and Publicity Director.

Architecture: Architect, City Planner, Landscape Architect, Drafting Specialist, Model Maker, Lighting Consultant, Letterer and Architectural Illustrator.

Cinematography: Cinematographer, Photographer, Computer Programmer, Animator, Set Designer, Make-Up Artist, Camera Person, Special Effects Person, Director, Choreographer, Costume Designer, Cutter/Editor, Lighting Consultant and Graphic Artist.

Criminology: Police Artist, Police/Legal Photographer, Private Investigator and Crime Lab Technician.

Education: Computer Teacher, Art Teacher, Industrial Arts Teacher, Vocational Education Teacher, Art Therapist, Textbook Author, Researcher, Artist-In-Residence, Journalism Teacher, Media/AV Specialist, Drama Teacher and Librarian.

Fashion: Haut Couturier, Fashion Illustrator, Fashion Editor/Designer, Hair Stylist, Make-Up Consultant, Photographer, Jewelry Designer, Commentator, Color Consultant, Window Decorator, Buyer and Dressmaker.

Fine Arts and Crafts: Painter, Sculptor, Printmaker, Photographer, Art Film Maker, Portraitist, Muralist, Ceramicist, Jeweler Designer, Weaver, Leather Craftsman, Metalworker, Cabinet Maker, Stained-Glass Designer, Woodcarver and Serigrapher.

Galleries: Gallery Director/Owner, Curator, Art Librarian, Restorer, Researcher, Gallery School Instructor, Guide, Lecturer, Art Dealer, Artists' Agent, Salesperson and Display Artist.

Industry and Business: Industrial Designer, Art Director, Design Consultant, Industrial Photographer, Typography Designer, Computer Programmer, Drafting Specialist, Market Researcher, Textile Designer, Foundry Artist, Package Designer, Design Engineer, Exhibition/Display Designer, Tool Designer, Mock-Up Artist, Buyer, Sign Painter and Model Maker.

Interior Design: Interior Designer, Decorating Studio Assistant, Color/Lighting/Fabric Consultant, Upholsterer, Model Maker, Illustrator, Antique Restorer and Furniture Designer.

Journalism and Publishing: Computer Programmer, Art Editor, Illustrator, Cartoonist, Graphic Designer, Photographer, Photo Retoucher, Layout Artist, Calligrapher, Greeting Card Designer, Photography Editor and Political Cartoonist.

Military: Training Aids Artist, Cartographer, Combat Photographer, Drafting Specialist, Aerial Photographer, Combat Artist, Weapon Designer, Computer Programmer.

Photography: Portrait Photographer, Photo Journalist, Fashion Photographer, News Photographer, Video Camera Person, Dark Room Technician, Industrial Photographer, Commercial Photographer.

Science and Museums: Technical Illustrator, Medical Illustrator, Scientific Photographer, Curator, Display Artist, Diorama Artist, Field Expedition Artist, Marine Illustrator and Museum School Instructor.

Learner Outcomes or Objectives

1. The student will demonstrate an ability to complete visual patterns during partnering and/or group activities.

2. The student will demonstrate an ability to use appropriate social skills while participating in visual problem solving activities during partnering and/or group activities.

3. The student will use convergent and divergent visual thinking skills to gather data for the completion of assignments.

4. The student will evidence an ability to visually analyze and synthesize data during creative problem solving activities.

5. The student will evidence an ability to combine visual thinking and divergent questioning skills to apply, analyze, synthesize and evaluate printed materials to accomplish learning activities.

6. The student will evidence a measurable improvement in spatial thinking from participating in daily visual thinking activities.

7. The student will use graphic organizers, mindMaps or webs to demonstrate visual thinking skills.

8. The student will use graphic organizers, mindMaps or webs to depict visually two remote or uncommon ideas.

9. The student will demonstrate an ability to appreciate the feelings and point of view of others by responding to visual and spatial stimulation.

10. The student will use visual thinking skills to develop a more positive self esteem by recognizing and using his/her abilities, becoming more self-directed and appreciating likenesses and differences between himself/herself and others.

11. The student will learn the language of visual thinking by completing visual puzzles and patterns every day.

12. The student will evidence an improvement in attention span, concentration and focusing ability through the practice of visual thinking.

13. The student will evidence an improvement in patience, perseverance and tolerance for frustration through the practice of visual thinking.

14. The "At Risk" student will evidence an improvement in listening skills and short term memory by practicing visual thinking.

15. The gifted and talented student will evidence an improvement in flexible, high level thinking by practicing visual thinking.

16. The student will use visual problem solving skills to develop ideas related to broad-based issues or themes.

17. The student will use active visual thinking by creating an original worksheet, model or other original product.

18. The student will use visual thinking to complete an independent study project that is unique.

19. The student will generate original visual images or symbols related to a topic or idea.

20. The student will brainstorm many pictures, symbols or images that fit different categories.

21. The student will effectively interpret and use nonverbal forms of thinking (visual thinking) to express his/her ideas, feelings and needs to others.

22. The student will place examples of original visual thinking and visual problem solving in a personal portfolio to show evidence of mastery.

23. The student will use active questioning techniques to describe a visual image or picture.

24. The student will predict many different causes/effects for given visual situations and/or problems.

25. The student will combine visual thinking and kinesthetic thinking to evidence improved critical thinking skills.

26. The student will show evidence of high level, critical thinking by combining intellectual, emotional and kinesthetic learning.

27. The student will make visual forced associations by combining two or more dissimilar images.

The Language of Visual Thinking

Pattern Completion: The completion of visual drawings, pictures, arrangements, configurations or patterns.

Sequencing Visually: Identifying and extending visual, progressive, incremental patterns.

Analytical Seeing: Identifying the basic elements or parts of what is being seen through visual analysis and estimation.

Synthesizing Visually: Being able to take parts of what is seen and putting them together to form "wholes."

Visual Recall: Learning to see clearly, in detail, and retain the image.

Multi-Sensory Imagery: Developing images from sounds, colors, tastes, smells and touch.

Once the above skills are understood, students will be able to integrate them to master the following **concepts**:

Congruences
Directionality
Patterns
Dimension
Position
Part/Whole Relationships
Giving and Following Directions

Diagramming
Ordering
Depth Perception
Reproduction
MindMapping
Symmetry
Comparing/Contrasting
Reflection

Magnitude of Length, Height, Distance, Volume
Using and Understanding Geometric Shapes and Models

Learning

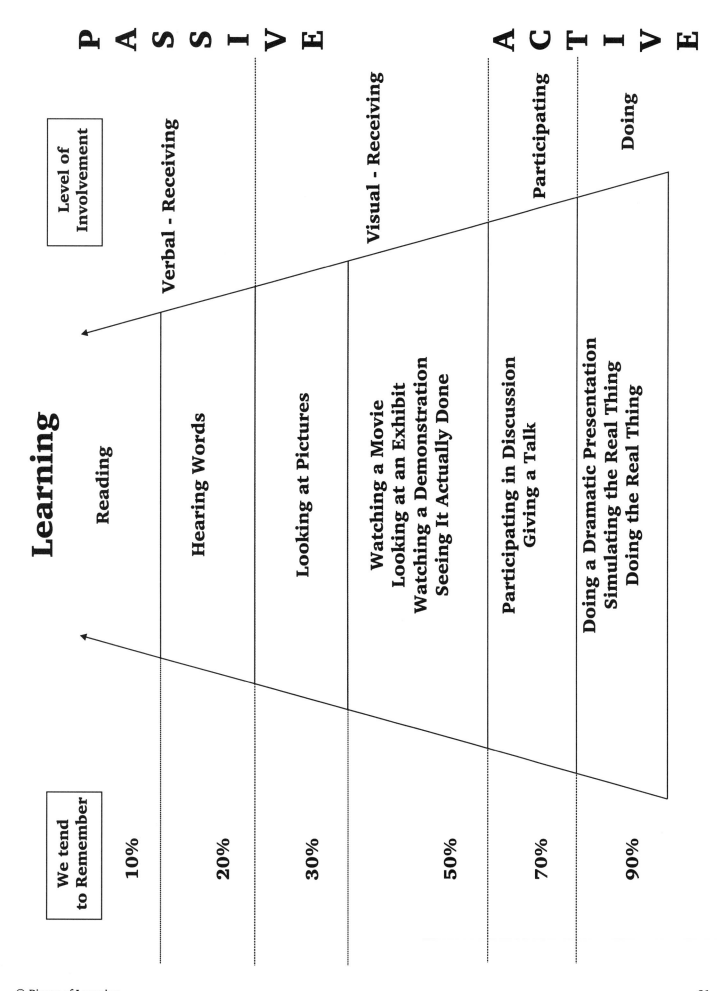

PASSIVE		Level of Involvement		We tend to Remember
	Reading			10%
Verbal - Receiving	Hearing Words			20%
	Looking at Pictures			30%
Visual - Receiving	Watching a Movie Looking at an Exhibit Watching a Demonstration Seeing It Actually Done			50%
ACTIVE **Participating**	Participating in Discussion Giving a Talk			70%
Doing	Doing a Dramatic Presentation Simulating the Real Thing Doing the Real Thing			90%

How To Use The Activities In This Book

The Teacher: Your attitude says it all. Visual thinking needs an open, accepting environment. You have to work at making it learner friendly. Your students must understand the significance and importance of using good visual skills in their lives, but they must also have fun doing it. Try building a visual activity or visual skill builder into every lesson plan. Start the day or period with a readiness activity that is visual. Go slow. A little visual stuff each day is better than a quick, concentrated unit. Remember! If you think visual thinking is really important, so will your students.

Each type of visual thinking in this book begins with easy examples then continues with more difficult ones. The pattern of easy to hard must always be closely maintained. A little frustration is good. Too much frustration will cause a major "melt down" in motivation.

Each type of thinking **always** ends in ACTIVE visual thinking. For the student, PASSIVE visual thinking happens when the teacher provides the visual examples, questions and lessons. ACTIVE visual thinking happens when students make up, create or draw their own visual ideas. That's the real purpose of this book——to encourage students to do their own visual thinking. All of the ACTIVE visual thinking pages are labeled **student made**. They make excellent examples for STUDENT PORTFOLIOS. Why not label one section of a student's portfolio Visual Thinking? That will encourage the continuous practice that visual thinking requires. It will also validate its importance to parents as they view their child's portfolio on conference day.

The Classroom: An overhead projector is a must. Many of the easiest and least expensive visual activities can be done by simply turning them into transparencies. (This book is meant to be USED! Tear it apart! Turn all the pages into transparencies.) When the overhead projector is used, students are forced to use visual thinking as the primary problem solving device.

Take a long, critical look at your classroom. Pretend you are the Visual Thinking Patrol. Just how "visual" is your classroom? Is it "visual friendly?" Is there too much visual stimulation in your classroom? Lots of clutter is not the same as lots of detail. Open space or "white space" on the walls is important too. More is not the same as different.

The "Four-Corner" Visual Classroom

If Nancy Johnson ruled the world, (Thank goodness she really doesn't!) every classroom would have four special tables in it—one in each corner of the room.

Table ONE should have checkers and chess games available for impromptu practice sessions. After students finish their required assignments, they can go to a corner of their classroom and play checkers or chess instead of doing two more worksheets. Both games are wonderful visual thinking tools. Patterning, concentration, problem solving and memory skills are stimulated with every move. Players with similar abilities will quickly find each other. Tournaments can be organized depending on the maturity of the players and the amount of competition the teacher wants to promote.

Table TWO should have a jigsaw puzzle on it; one of those 1000 piece models. Jigsaw puzzles are pure visual problem solving. It takes concentration, focus, patience and perseverance to find that certain missing piece. And the jigsaw puzzle has come a long way since the days when one covered the dining room table in the Johnson family farm house. Today there are jigsaw puzzles that have hidden clues to a mystery. Others are three dimensional. Still others lack borders (no straight sides!) with extra pieces that won't fit anywhere. Also, don't underestimate the power that jigsaw puzzles have in stimulating communication. More than one problem or misunderstanding has been discussed, mediated and solved at the puzzle table.

Table THREE should have a big sign that says, **Make It Visual!** Stock it with the following arts and crafts materials: markers, pens, colored pencils, paint, glue, tape, scissors, stapler, paper clips, rubber bands, yarn, feathers, old wallpaper books, construction paper, cloth, buttons, beads, popsicle sticks, pipe cleaners and string. Enhance book reports, creative writing assignments and projects of all kinds with color, pictures, posters, collages, drawings and sculptures.

Table FOUR should have at least one computer. It would be connected to a school-wide network so teachers and students could receive E-mail as well as run various software programs. When it comes to visual thinking and visual problem solving the two best are THE FACTORY and INSPIRATION®.

THE FACTORY/La Fabrica

Grades: 4-adult
Designed by: Marge Cappo and Mike Fish, WINGS For Learning

Awards: Best Software of the Year, Learning; Best of the Decade, Classroom Computer Learning
Recommended by: Booklist, Electronic Learning and Parents' Choice

Students are challenged to make products by using machines that punch, rotate, and stripe in a simulated factory assembly line. They will develop insights into spatial relationships, rotation, pattern, and sequence as they experiment and explore various possibilities with a variety of geometric shapes.

One disk, backup (IBM, Tandy, and Apple), teacher's guide.
Available on preview CD. Specs available: 1-800-321-7511
Site Licenses available. Spanish version available.

Order from: SUNBURST, Dept. CG99, 101 Castleton Street, PO Box 100, Pleasantville, NY 10570 1-800-321-7511 or FAX 914-747-4109

INSPIRATION®
A Unique Collaboration of Visual and Logical Thinking
Inspiration® Software Inc.
Portland Oregon

Visual and text-oriented thinkers find this program a useful writing and illustration tool. It allows working in graphic or text mode creating mindMaps, organizing outlines, and developing written products. Notes of text attach to symbols and appear on the outline! Great for random thinkers to create order to ideas for better writing products. Easy to master. Spell checker, tutorial, guided lessons, Idea Book, and Teacher Guide.

Take advantage of Rapid Fire brainstorming of ideas. One keystroke moves from mindMap to outline and mindMap to text mode. "Take" notes and hide them in mindmap symbols——recall them, edit them, print them! Choose from hundreds of mindMap symbols or import your own. Work in text mode or export to your word processor! For Mac and Windows - $89.00.

Order from: Pieces of Learning, 1610 Brook Lynn Drive, Beavercreek, OH 45432-1906
937-427-0530   1- 800-729-5137   Fax: 937-427-3380

Call for site licensing for your computer network.

An example of what Inspiration® can do is on the following page.

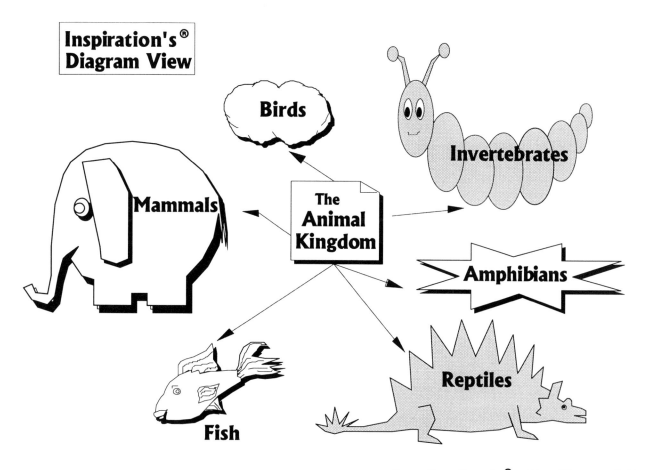

Inspiration's® Diagram View

Birds

Invertebrates

Mammals

The Animal Kingdom

Amphibians

Fish

Reptiles

Inspiration's® Outline with notes displayed

The Animal Kingdom
I. Mammals

Mammals produce milk, are found all over the world, live in the air, water, and land, are warm-blooded, and have hair and a backbone.

II. Amphibians

Amphibians are animals that live on land and in water. Frogs, toads, salamanders, and newts are examples.

III. Fish

Fish have fins and live in water.

IV. Reptiles

Examples of reptiles are snakes, turtles, lizards, and crocodiles.

V. Birds

Birds have feathers, wings, and are warm-blooded.

VI. Invertebrates

There are more invertebrates than any other animal. They don't have backbones. All other animals do.

Inspiration's® Outline View

The Animal Kingdom
I. Mammals
II. Amphibians
III. Fish
IV. Reptiles
V. Birds
VI. Invertebrates

To order the educational version of Inspiration® for Mac or Windows: Call
Pieces of Learning **1-800-729-5137**
$89 plus S/H

MindMapping: The VISUAL Way To Outline

MindMapping provides a visual framework for ideas. It can be teacher or student generated. In the beginning, the teacher presents completed mindMaps as examples to the students. Ultimately, the students themselves draw and use their own mindMaps. Simply stated, mindMapping is a visual alternative to traditional methods of outlining.

In her book, **It's About Writing** (Pieces of Learning, 1990), Kathy Balsamo does an excellent job explaining mindMapping.

1. The middle of each mindMap is called the **FOCUS**. Like a word association game, a question is asked. "What do you think of when you think of (focus)?" It might be a prediction question. "What would happen if (focus) could not talk?"

2. Each line from the **FOCUS** is called a **BRIDGE**. Sometimes adjectives or adverbs which relate to the **FOCUS** are written on the **BRIDGE**.

3. The **BRIDGE** connects the **FOCUS** to the **LINK**, the circle in which the answer to the question is placed.

The mindMap grows larger as more questions, ideas and responses are considered.

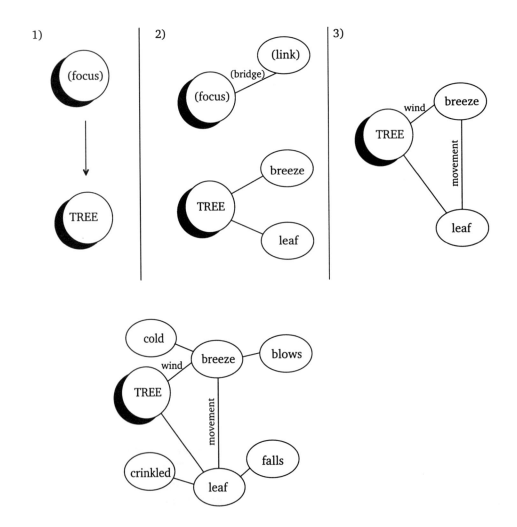

Science Curriculum Planning
Using Mindmapping

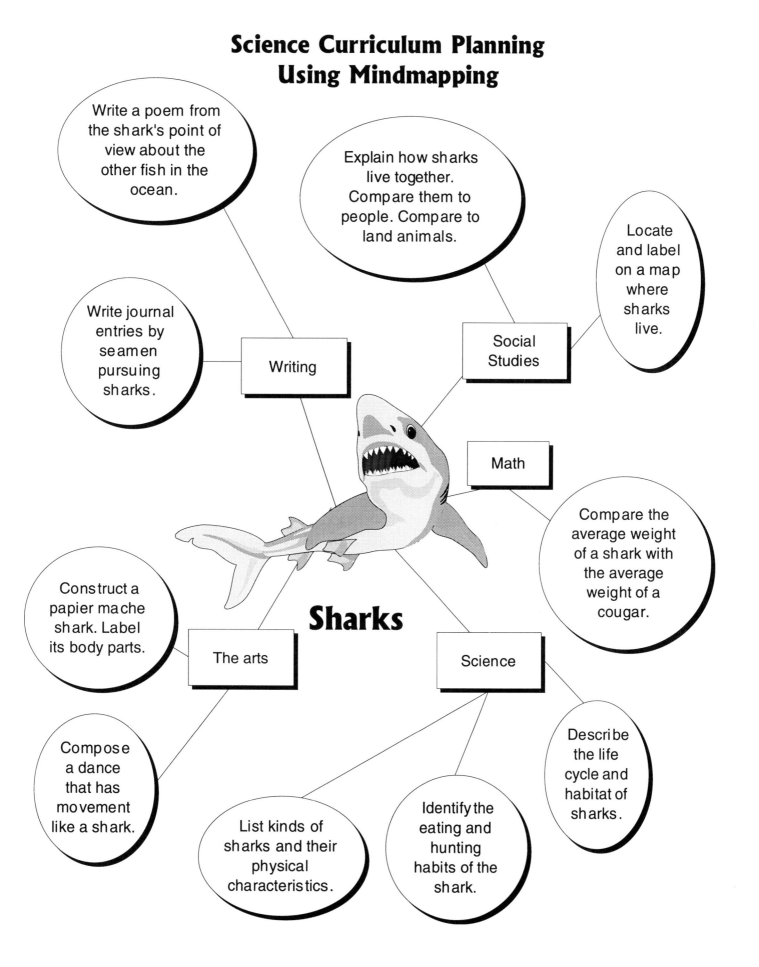

Write a poem from the shark's point of view about the other fish in the ocean.

Explain how sharks live together. Compare them to people. Compare to land animals.

Locate and label on a map where sharks live.

Write journal entries by seamen pursuing sharks.

Writing

Social Studies

Math

Compare the average weight of a shark with the average weight of a cougar.

Construct a papier mache shark. Label its body parts.

The arts

Science

Sharks

Describe the life cycle and habitat of sharks.

Compose a dance that has movement like a shark.

List kinds of sharks and their physical characteristics.

Identify the eating and hunting habits of the shark.

Name _Steve B._   **Topic** _Science - Sharks_

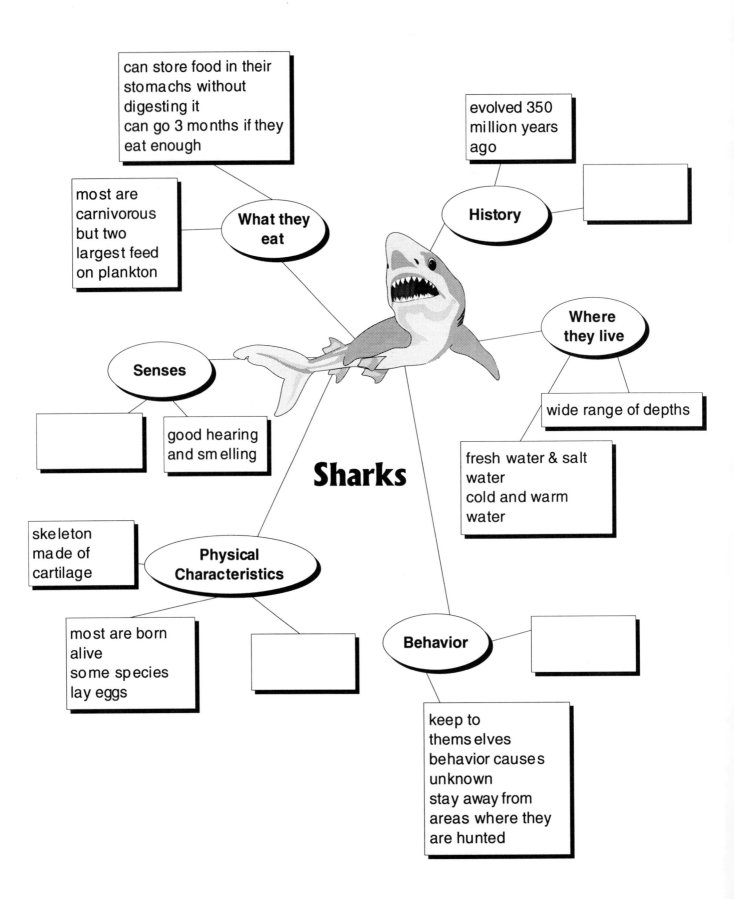

can store food in their stomachs without digesting it
can go 3 months if they eat enough

evolved 350 million years ago

most are carnivorous but two largest feed on plankton

What they eat

History

Where they live

Senses

good hearing and smelling

wide range of depths

fresh water & salt water
cold and warm water

Sharks

skeleton made of cartilage

Physical Characteristics

most are born alive
some species lay eggs

Behavior

keep to themselves
behavior causes unknown
stay away from areas where they are hunted

Curriculum Planning
Using Mindmapping

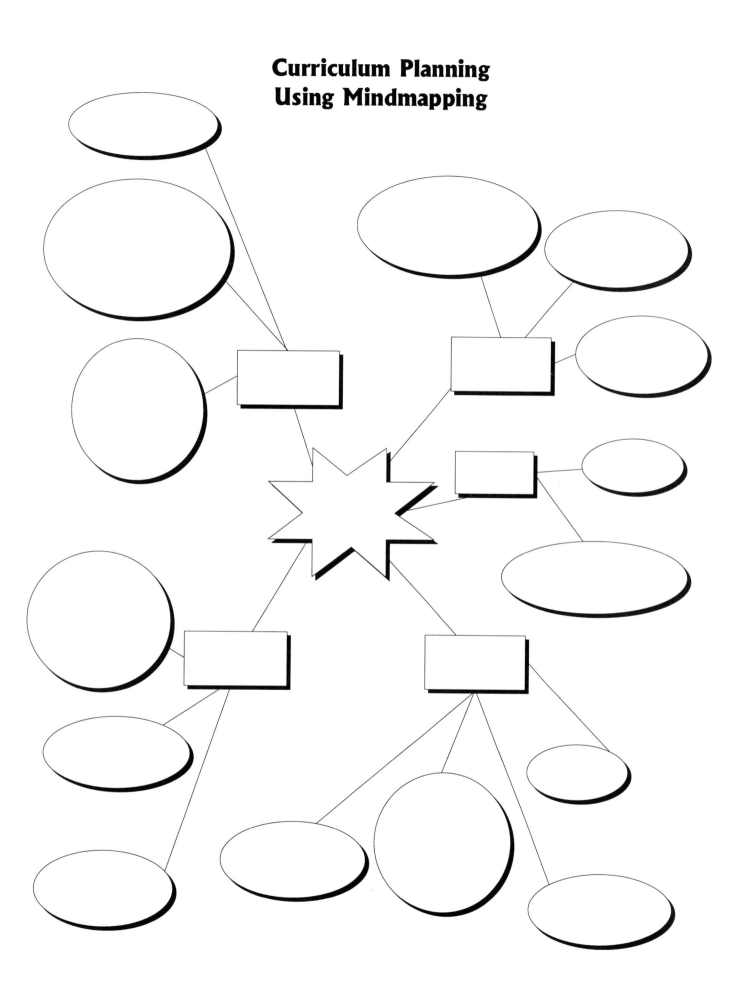

LOOK CLOSER AT
OPTICAL ILLUSIONS

2

Which of the two circles in the center is larger?

1

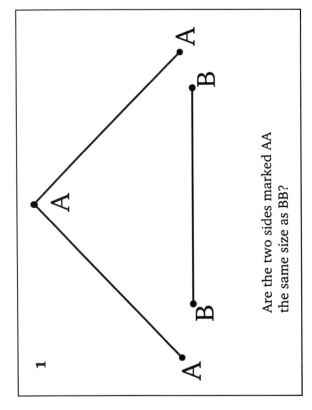

Are the two sides marked AA the same size as BB?

4

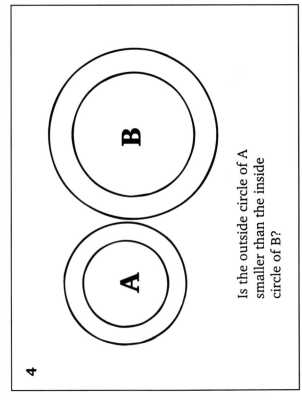

Is the outside circle of A smaller than the inside circle of B?

3

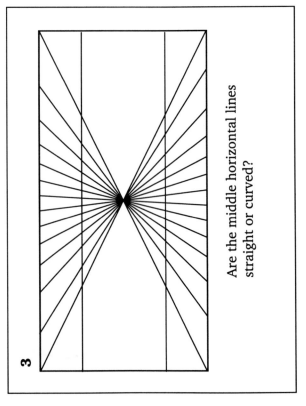

Are the middle horizontal lines straight or curved?

MULLER-LYER ILLUSIONS

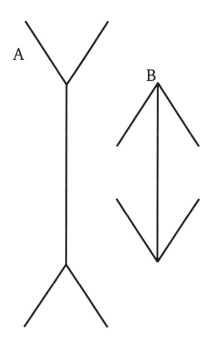

Are the vertical lines
in A and B the same length?

Are the top
and bottom parts
of the verical line
the same length?

Are the top
and bottom parts
of the vertical
line the same
length?

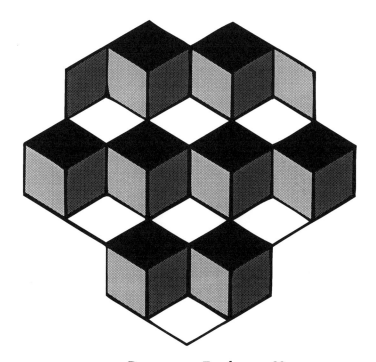

Do you see 7 cubes or 8?

What do you see?

Analytical Seeing/Visualization

In each box, is there more black or more white?

Analytical Seeing/Visualization

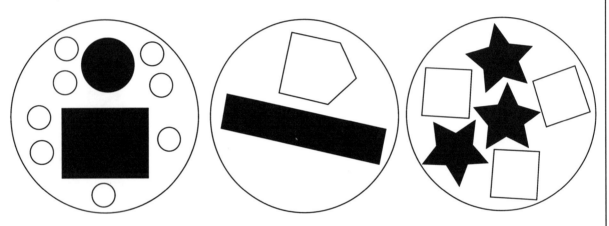

Look at the shapes inside each circle. Is there more black or more white?

Analytical Seeing/Visualization

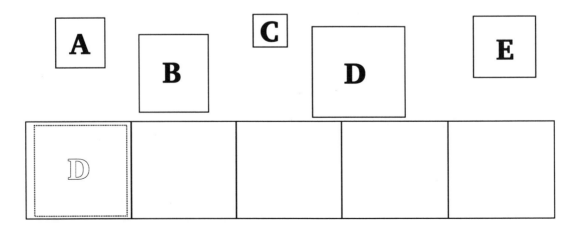

Draw the boxes in order, from the largest to smallest.

ACTIVE VISUAL THINKING

Analytical Seeing/Visualization

In each box, is there more _____ or more _____?

Analytical Seeing/Visualization

In each circle, is there more _____ or more _____?

Analytical Seeing/Visualization

Draw the _____ in order, from the largest to the smallest.

PUZZLE POWER!

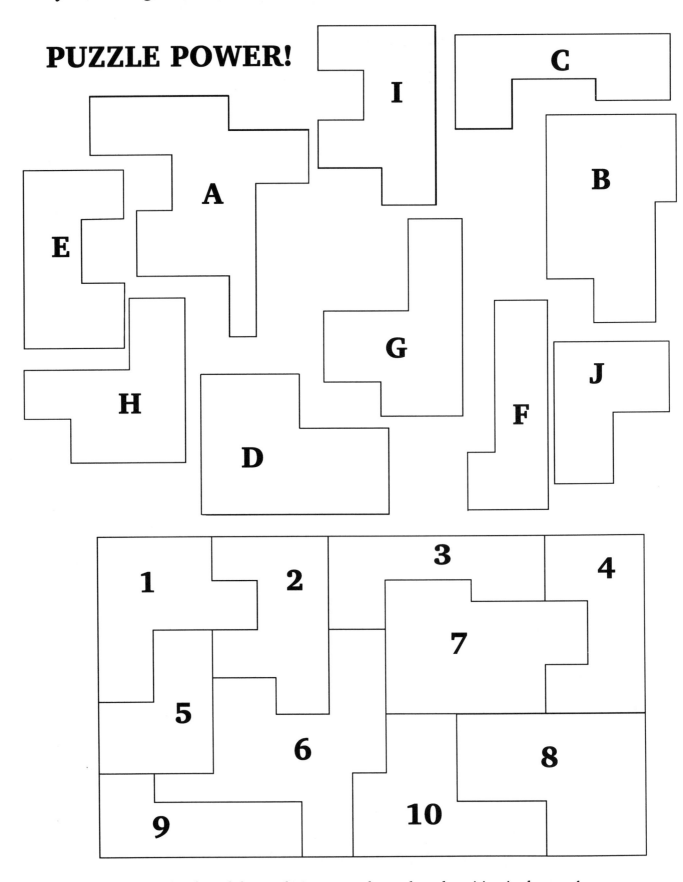

Match each lettered piece to each numbered position in the puzzle.

Active Visual Thinking
PUZZLE POWER!

Draw a lined puzzle and number each piece.

Draw puzzle pieces from above and letter them.

Match each lettered piece to each numbered position in the puzzle.
Remember! Do it with your eyes! After you have matched each piece
with your eyes, THEN you may cut out each one and lay it on top of the puzzle.

VISUAL CALISTHENICS

Follow the folding of the paper with your eyes.

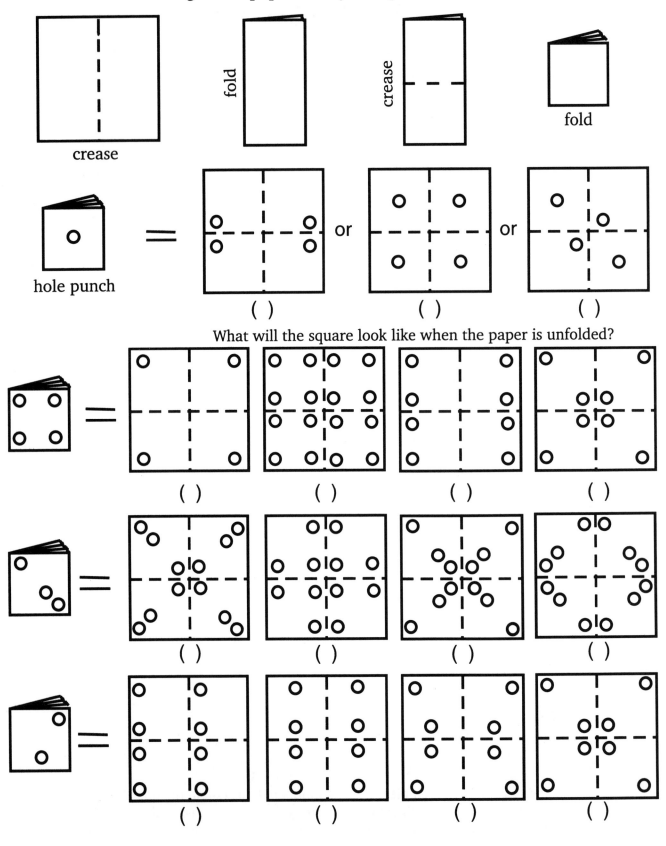

What will the square look like when the paper is unfolded?

MORE VISUAL CALISTHENICS

Follow the folding of the paper with your eyes.

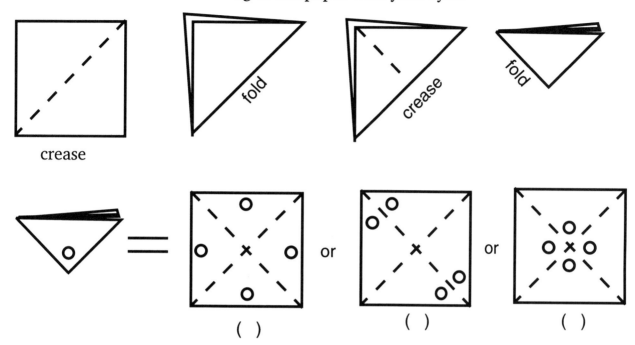

What will the square look like when the paper is unfolded?

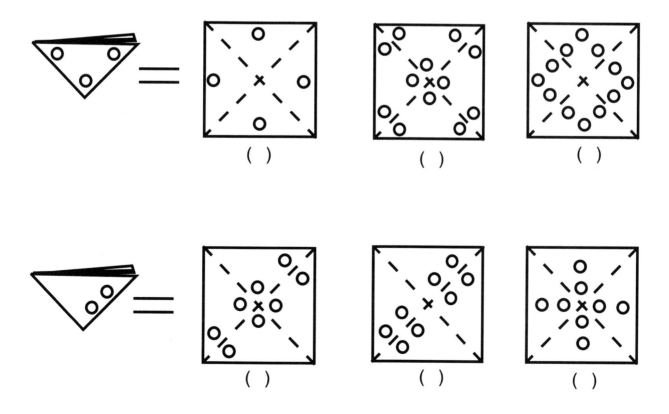

MORE VISUAL CALISTHENICS

Follow the **unfolding** of the paper with your eyes.

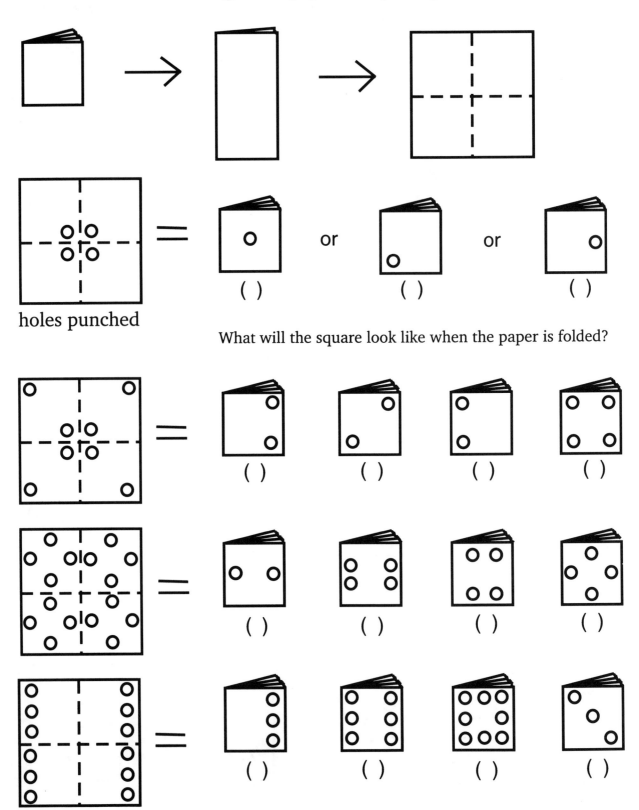

holes punched

What will the square look like when the paper is folded?

VISUAL CALISTHENICS

Follow the unfolding of the paper with your eyes.

GRID WORK!

Look closely at the pattern on the (A) grid. Study it carefully with your eyes!
First, practice "drawing" the pattern with your eyes on the (B) grid. Next,
draw the EXACT same pattern in the EXACT same location on the (B) grid.

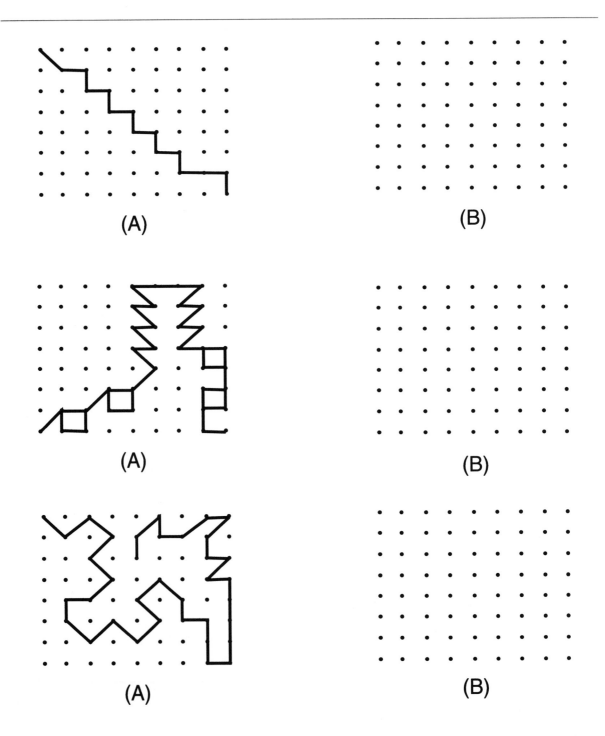

(A)   (B)

(A)   (B)

(A)   (B)

Active Visual Thinking
GRID WORK!

Draw a different line pattern on each (A) grid. Trade patterns with a friend. Complete the (B) grids by copying the EXACT same pattern in the EXACT same location.

(A)   (B)

(A)   (B)

(A)   (B)

THE DOTS HAVE IT!

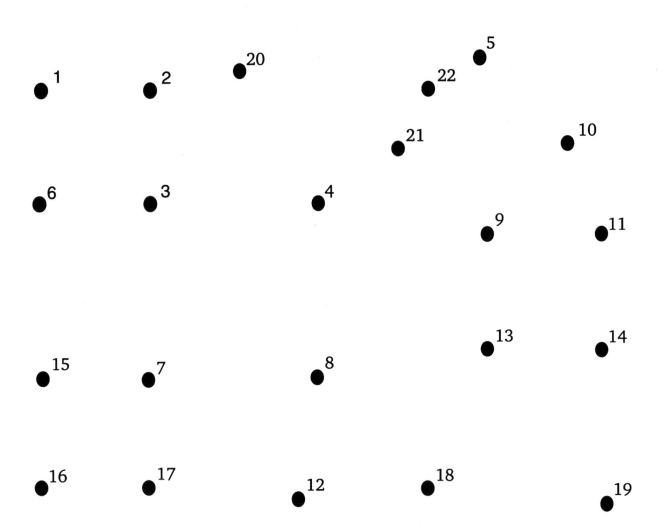

When the dots numbered 1, 2, 3, 6, and 1 are connected they form a square. Can you find more squares? Remember! A square must have four EQUAL sides. Use only your eyes. Don't use a pencil.

When the dots numbered 20, 21, 4, and 20 are connected they form a triangle. Can you find more triangles? Remember! A triangle has three sides. Use only your eyes. Don't use a pencil.

<u>   1, 2, 3, 6, 1   </u>

_____

_____

_____

squares

<u>   20, 21, 4, 20   </u>

_____

_____

_____

triangles

Active Visual Thinking

THE DOTS HAVE IT!

Create a numbered dot pattern with "hidden" shapes.

When the dots numbered _____ are connected they form a _____ .

When the dots numbered _____ are connected they form a _____ .

List other shapes and their numbers hidden in the dots.

Shapes	Dot Numbers
_____	_____
_____	_____
_____	_____
_____	_____

Shapes	Dot Numbers
_____	_____
_____	_____
_____	_____
_____	_____

HIDDEN WORDS

Write the hidden word in the blank.

HELLO   _____

SLIME   _____

ZERO   _____

QUACK   _____

GREEN   _____

JUMP   _____

HIDDEN WORDS

Create your own list of hidden words.

_____   _____

_____   _____

_____   _____

_____   _____

_____   _____

_____   _____

SPINNING CUBE

Study the following three views of the SAME cube. Look carefully at each side of the cube. Try to "see" in your imagination the sides that are hidden from view.

What is opposite the ?

What is opposite the ?

What is opposite the ?

What is opposite the ?

What is opposite the ?

What is opposite the ?

Active Visual Thinking
SPINNING CUBE

Study the following three views of the SAME cube. Draw a different symbol or picture on each side of the cube. You will need six DIFFERENT pictures. Trade papers with a friend. Ask your friend to look carefully at your paper and answer the questions about the cube.

What is opposite
           the _____?

What is opposite
           the _____?

What is opposite
           the _____?

What is opposite
           the _____?

What is opposite
           the _____?

What is opposite
           the _____?

MORE SPINNING CUBES

Look carefully at the patterns on the left side of the page. When each pattern is folded into a cube, what will it look like? Put an (X) by the correct cube.

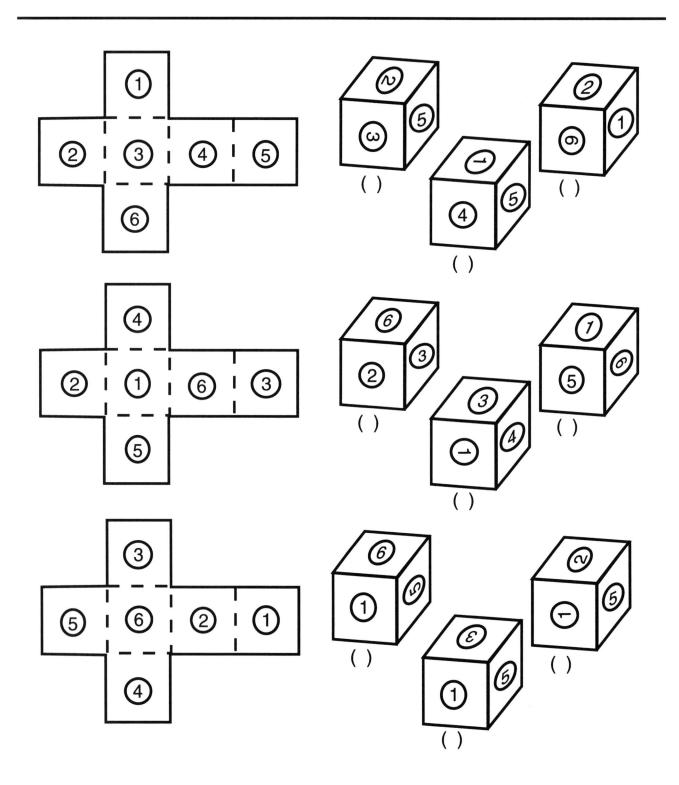

Active Visual Thinking
MORE SPINNING CUBES

Look carefully at the three unfolded cubes on the left side of the page. Each unfolded cube has six squares. Label each square with numbers, letters, pictures, or symbols. Each unfolded cube has three examples of folded cubes on the right side of the page. Label one folded cube correctly. Label the other two incorrectly. Trade papers with a friend. Ask your friend to look carefully at each cube and mark the one that is labeled correctly.

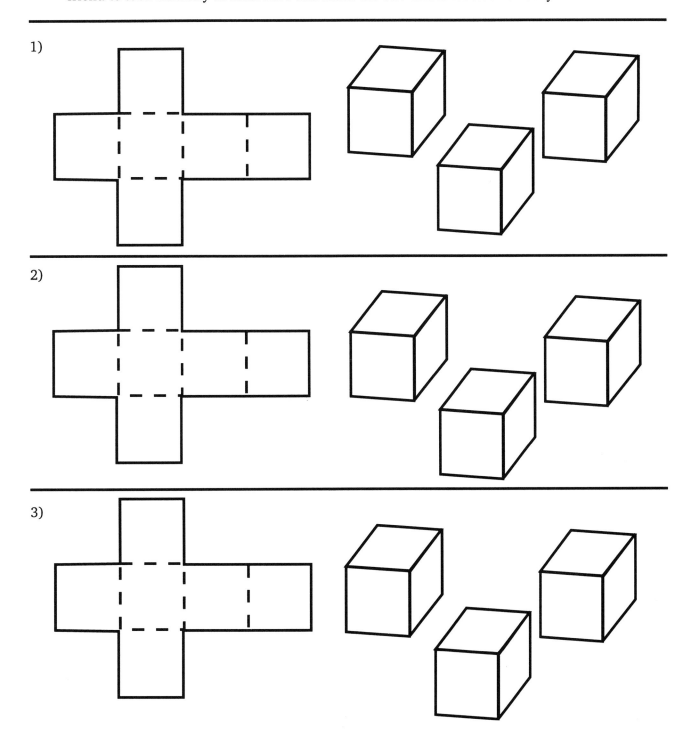

1)

2)

3)

Some students (and their teachers) may have trouble answering the questions about the SPINNING CUBE. Constructing a cube out of paper and labeling the sides combines visual thinking and kinesthetic thinking. When this pattern is cut out, creased, and taped together, it forms a cube. Each panel can be numbered or illustrated. Use the completed cube to answer the SPINNING CUBE questions.

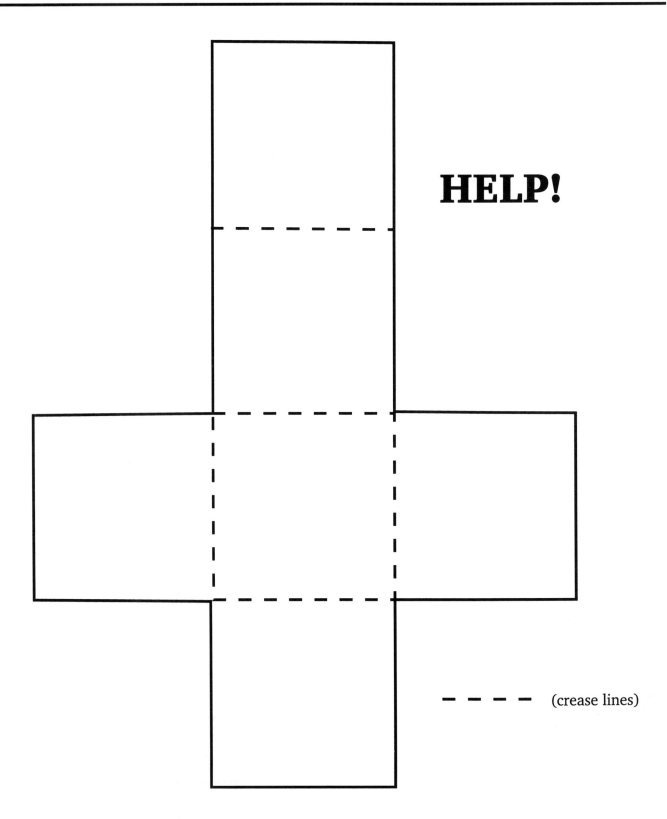

HELP!

− − − − (crease lines)

MEMORY BLOCKS

Organize students in partners or trios. Each student will need six or more wooden blocks, all a different color. The blocks should be one-inch cubes or larger. Kindergarten counting blocks will work fine, or sacks of wooden blocks can be ordered from:

Delta Education
P.O. Box 950
Hudson, NH   03051
1-800-442-5444

Most of the activities in this section are intended to be duplicated as transparencies for the overhead projector. Each group of two or three students has a small pile of blocks on a desk or table in front of them. The teacher/facilitator flashes each block pattern by turning the projector on and off as quickly as possible. Students duplicate the block pattern they have seen by rearranging their own blocks. The color of the blocks is not important—just the position.

Students are looking at a TWO-DIMENSIONAL block pattern on the screen that they must transform visually and kinesthetically to a THREE-DIMENSIONAL block pattern using their collection of wooden blocks.

NOTE: The patterns should be simple at first with a steady increase in difficulty. DO NOT allow students to stare at the patterns on the screen for several seconds. Two or three seconds, max! If they need a second or third look, give them another quick, two second flash. Visual recall and memory will be improved by combining quick flashes of a pattern with a steady increase in pattern difficulty.

After students have duplicated the pattern, the teacher/facilitator turns the projector on long enough for students to check to see if they have arranged the blocks correctly.

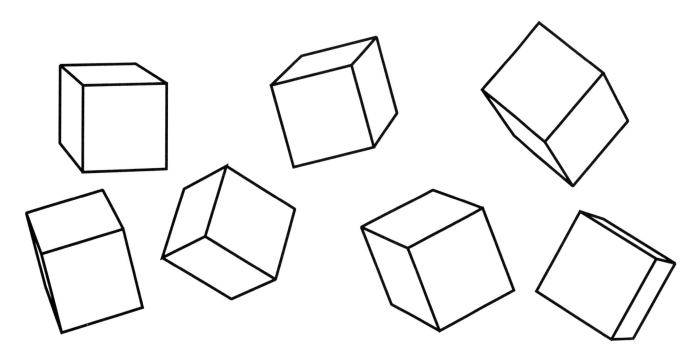

MEMORY BLOCKS

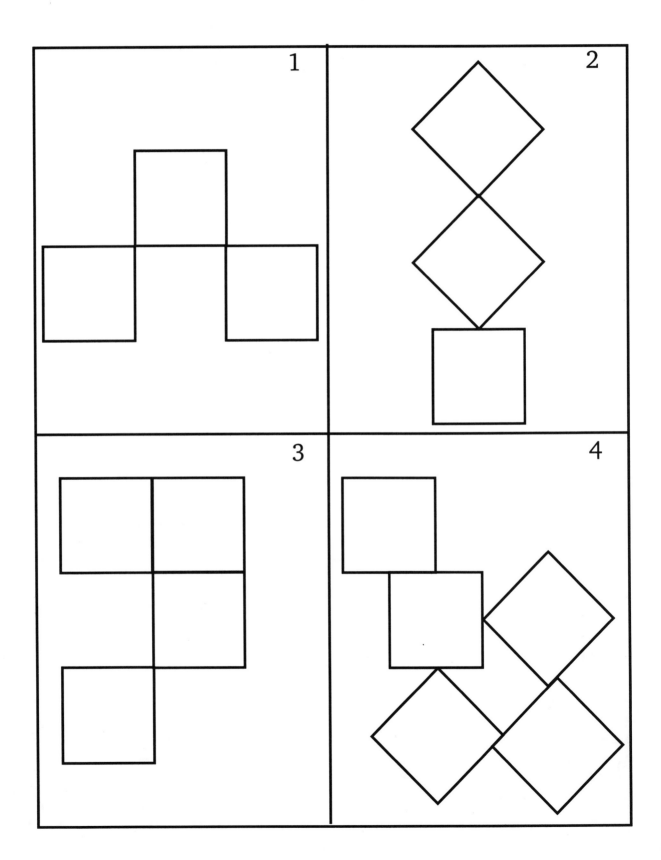

MEMORY BLOCKS

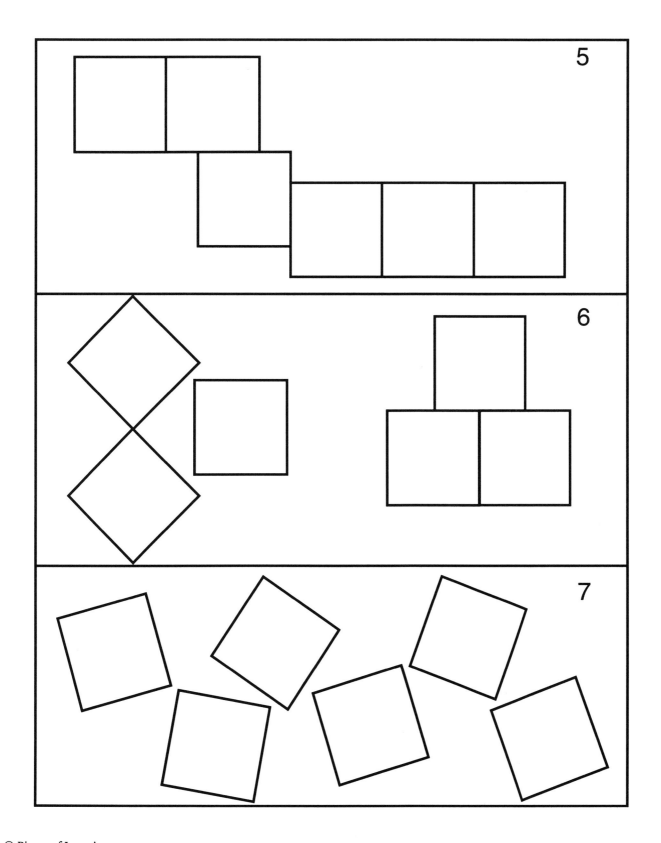

MEMORY BLOCKS

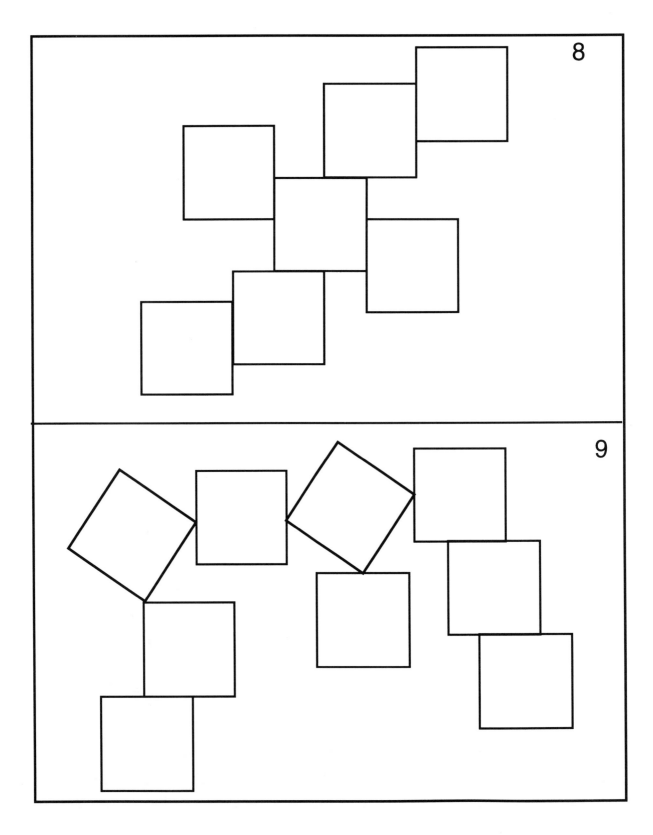

Active Visual Thinking
MEMORY BLOCKS

To the student: Trace around a one-inch wooden block to create your own memory block patterns. "Flash" the pattern to a friend. Can they duplicate your pattern?

BUILDING BLOCK PATTERNS

Duplicate the following pages as transparencies. The two-dimensional drawings are three views of the SAME structure built from one-inch wooden blocks. Place each transparency on the overhead projector. Allow students as much time as they need to look at the patterns. This is NOT a flashing exercise like the previous activities. Remind students several times that the views are of the SAME structure, just three different points of view. Leave the projector on the entire time so students can check their efforts as they try to transform the two-dimensional images into a three-dimensional structure. The patterns are progressively more difficult.

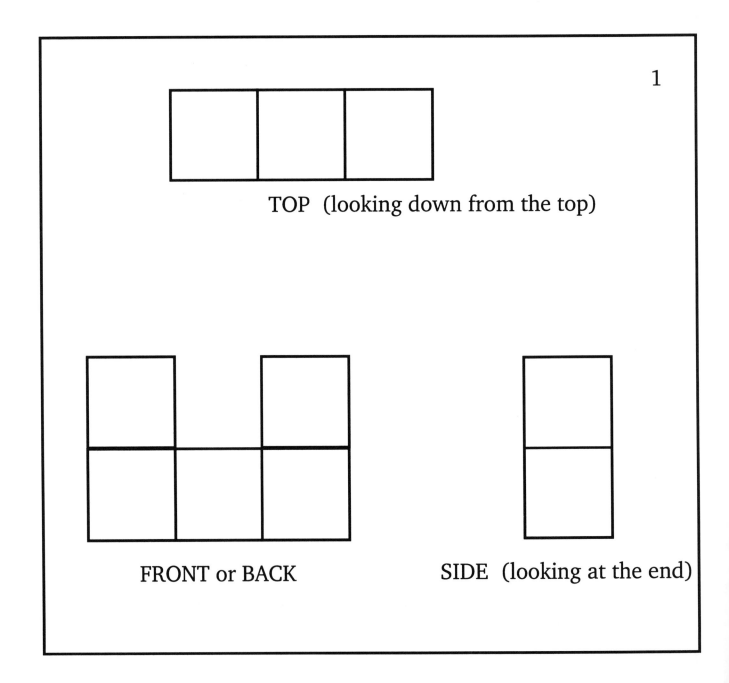

MORE BUILDING BLOCK PATTERNS

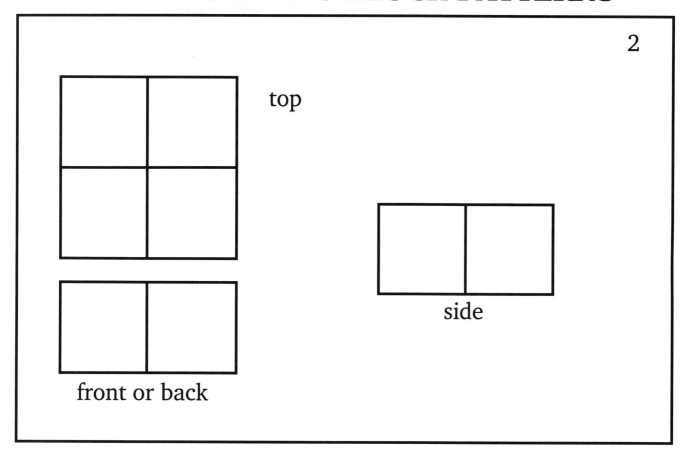

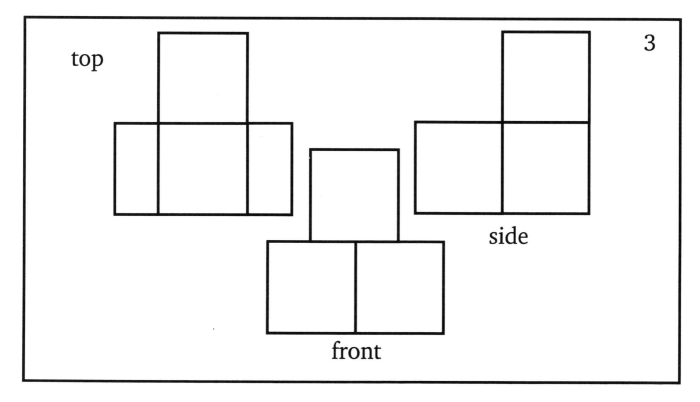

Active Visual Thinking
MORE BUILDING BLOCK PATTERNS

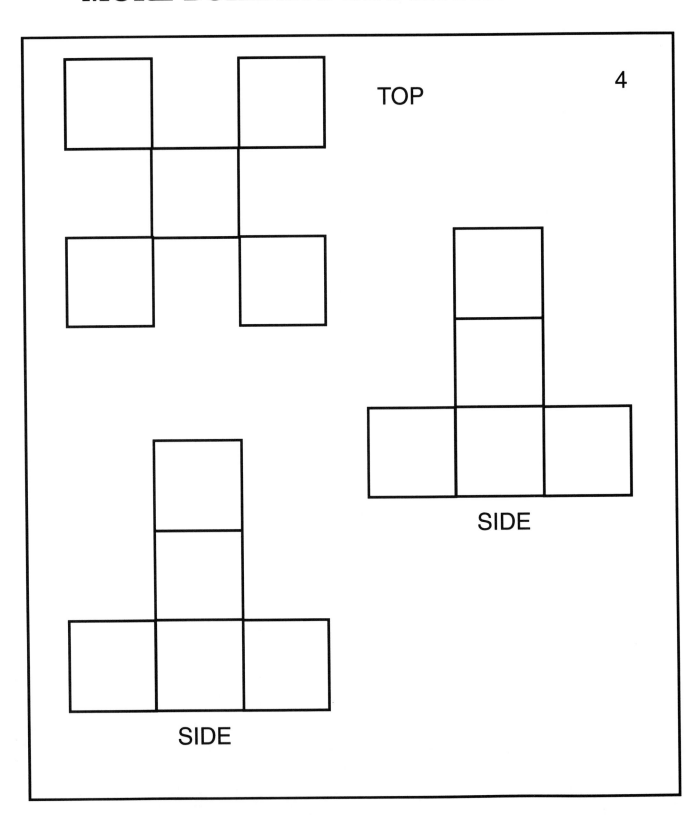

TOP

4

SIDE

SIDE

Active Visual Thinking

BLOCK PATTERN

To the student: Build a structure from one-inch wooden blocks. Make a two dimensional drawing of your design. (Use an extra block to trace around.) Remember! You must draw three views of the SAME structure. Label each view with the words *Top, Side,* or *Front*. Exchange your paper with a friend. Can your friend build the correct structure by looking at your drawing? Can you do the same by looking at your partner's drawing?

BUILDING IN THREE DIMENSIONS

Duplicate the following pages as transparencies. Place each transparency on the overhead. Allow students as much time as they need to look at the three-dimensional patterns. Leave the projector on the entire time so students can check their efforts. Surprise! Even though these patterns look more difficult, they will be much easier for many students because they are drawn as three-dimensional rather than two-dimensional. The patterns are progressively more difficult.

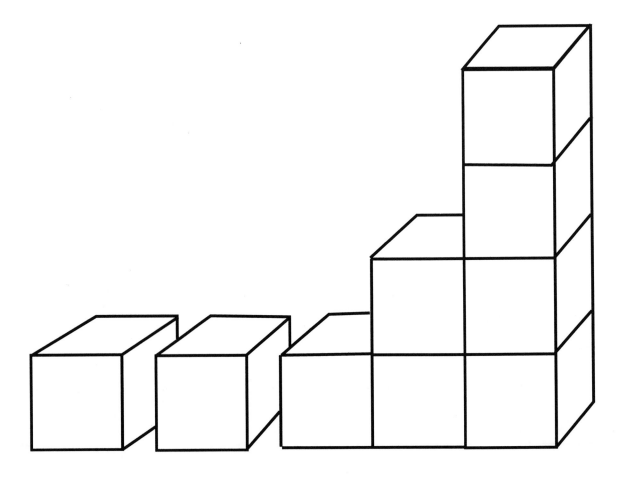

BUILDING IN THREE DIMENSIONS

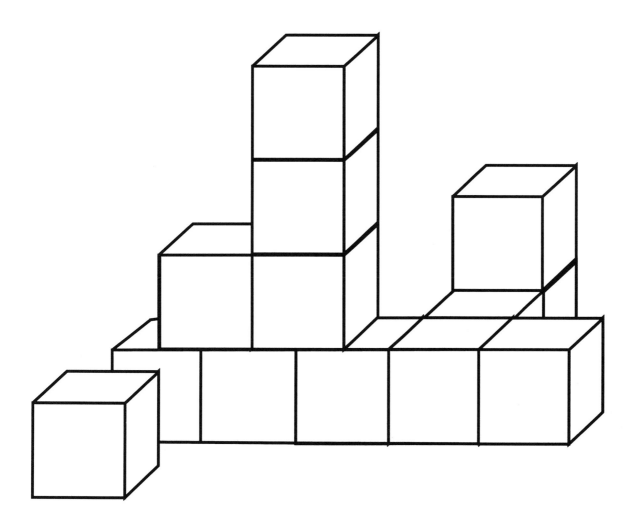

PIECE BY PIECE

STOP! Do not cut out the pieces of the puzzle with scissors. Instead, try cutting each piece out with your eyes. When the pieces are placed correctly they form a perfect frame around the cat. After you have tried to frame the cat with your eyes, then you may use the scissors to cut out each piece and place it correctly on the frame.

HERE KITTY KITTY!

Use your eyes to cover the worried cat. The five pieces below will do it!

TWO TOO MANY

Which two lettered pieces do not belong in the puzzle?

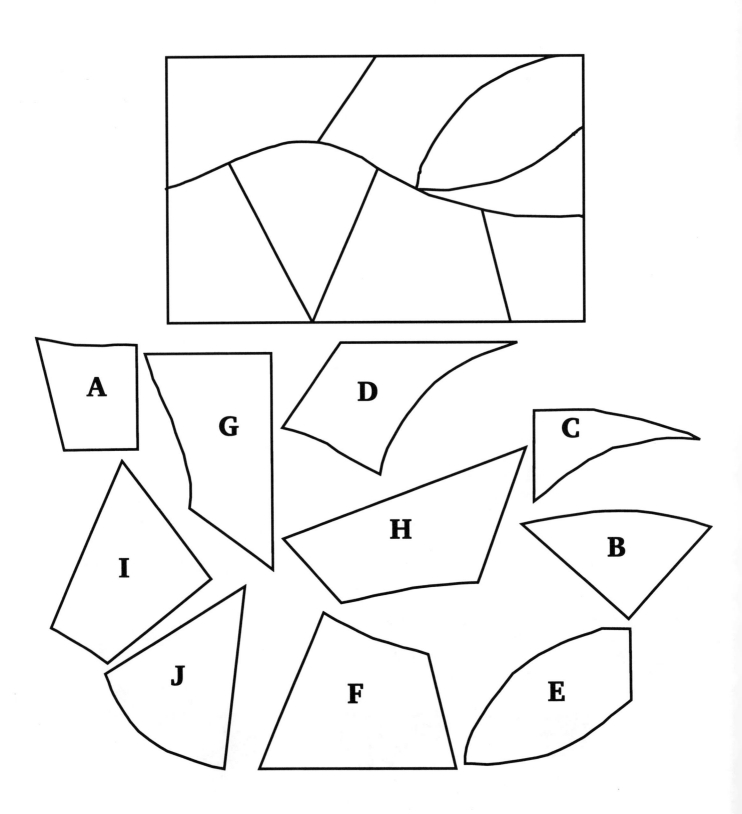

TWO TOO MANY

Which two lettered pieces do not belong in the puzzle?

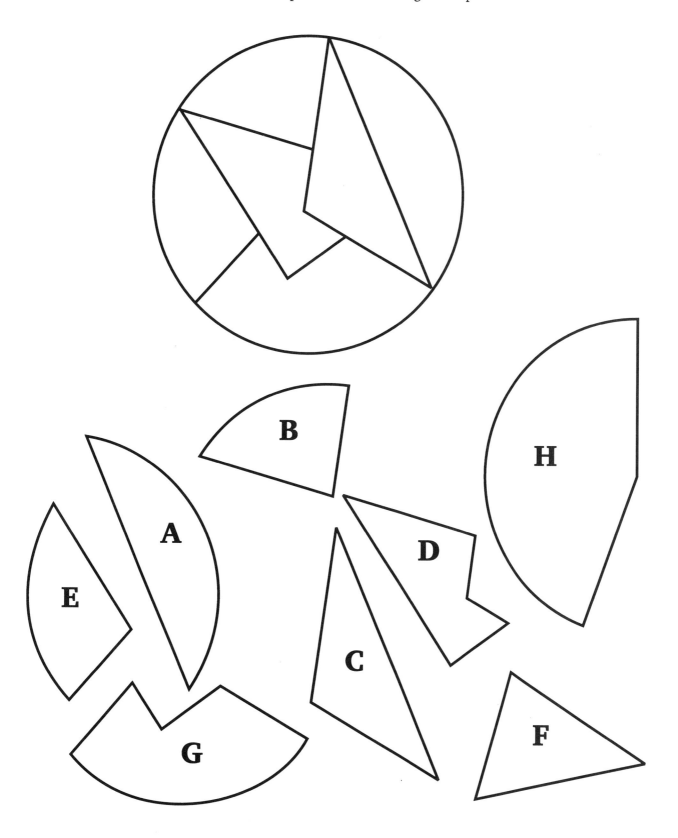

IS IT A KNOT OR NOT?

Use your eyes to pull the ends of each cord.
Which ones end up in a knot? Which ones don't?

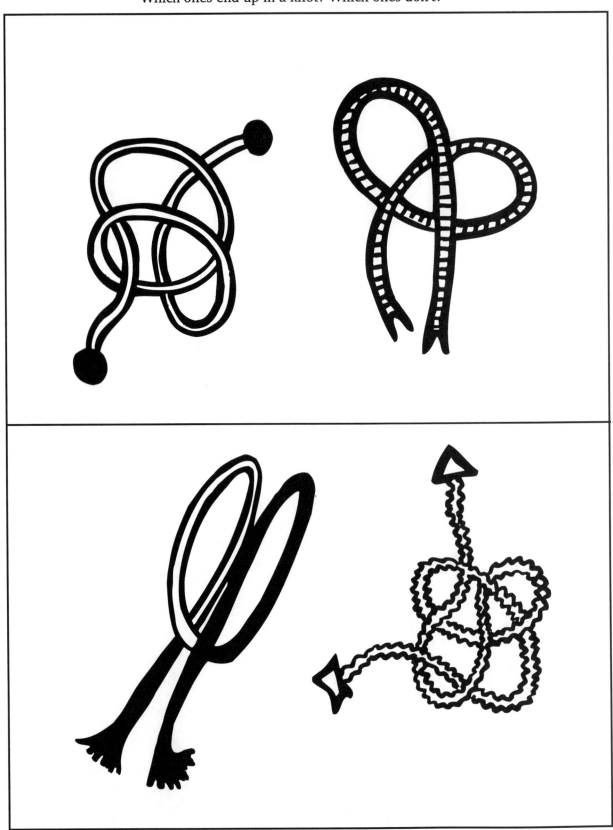

IS IT A KNOT OR NOT?

Draw 4 different cords. Give them to a friend and
see if they can determine if they are knots or not.

Matching Squares

Super Heroes!

Can you figure out where the nine squares below fit into the big picture? When you have finished, write a story about the adventures of these two super heroes.

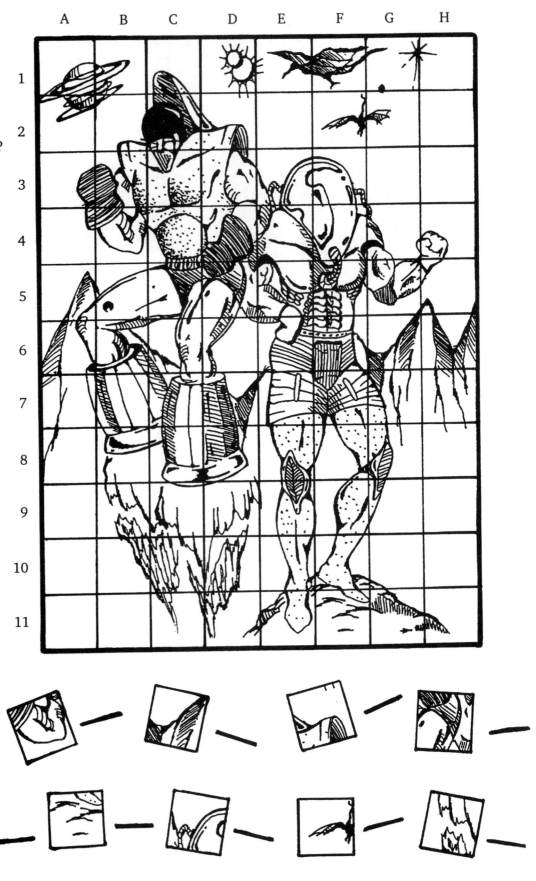

8E

Matching Squares

Rocket Man!

To create your own
"Matching Squares"
activity first ask your
teacher to make a copy of
the Rocket Man picture.
Then cut out 10 squares
and glue them in the entry
boxes at the bottom.

Challenge your friends to
find the squares in the
picture.

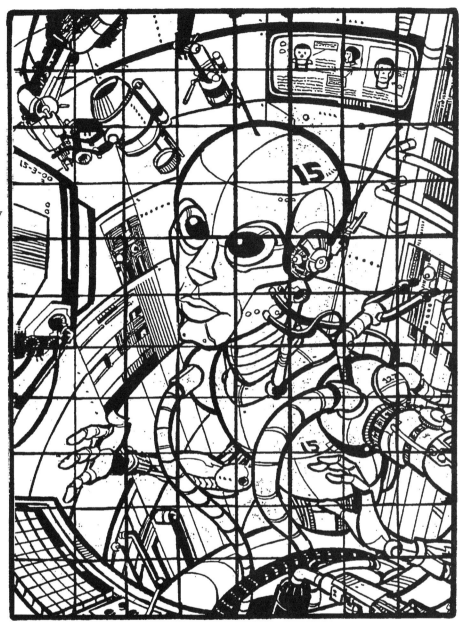

STAR BURST

Look at the four small examples and
then draw your own symmetrical design.

OOPS! WHAT'S MISSING?

Use a fine point black marker and
complete the pattern in each box.

GUESS-T-MATION

Stare at the gum ball machine for one minute. Try not to count each individual gum ball. Try to "see" the whole amount. Record your guesses, then count all the gum balls and compare the amounts.

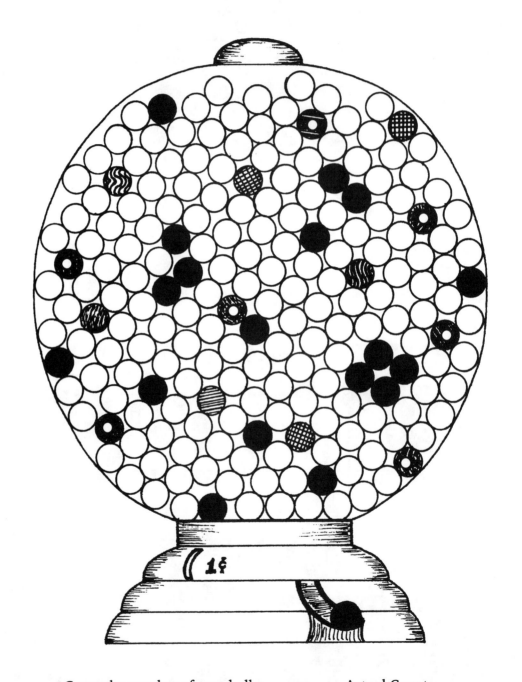

Guess the number of gum balls: _____   Actual Count: _____

Guess the number of black gum balls: _____   Actual Count: _____

GUESS-T-MATION

Guess the number of flies: _____

Actual Count: _____

GUESS-T-MATION

Fill the mouse with pieces of cheese. Ask a friend
to guess how many pieces fill the mouse.

Guess the number of pieces of cheese: _____

Actual Count: _____

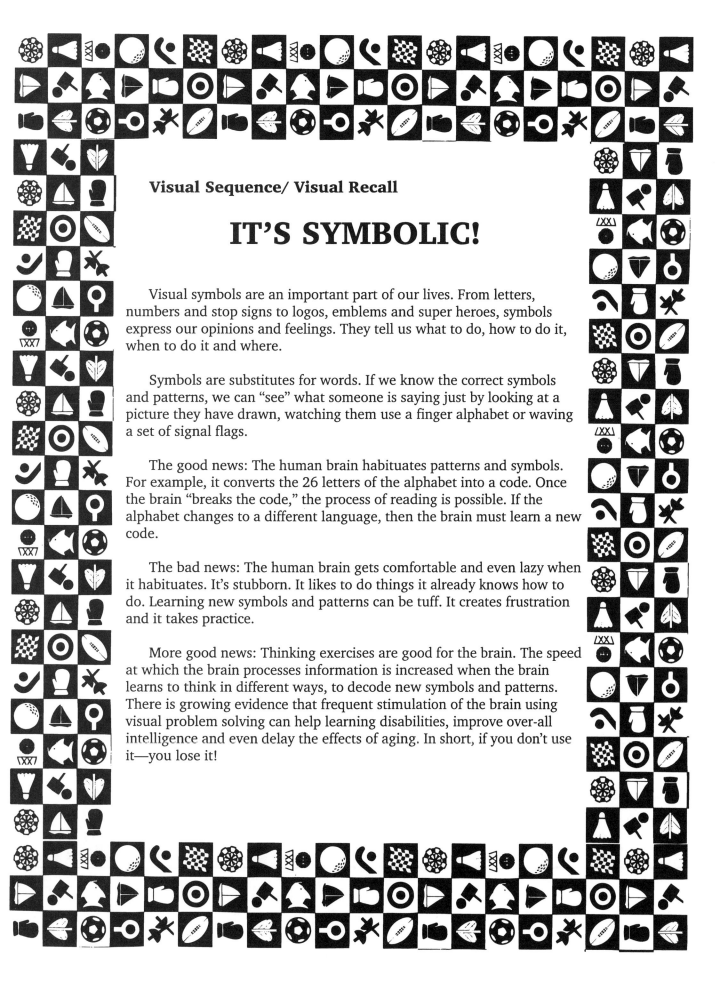

Visual Sequence/ Visual Recall

IT'S SYMBOLIC!

Visual symbols are an important part of our lives. From letters, numbers and stop signs to logos, emblems and super heroes, symbols express our opinions and feelings. They tell us what to do, how to do it, when to do it and where.

Symbols are substitutes for words. If we know the correct symbols and patterns, we can "see" what someone is saying just by looking at a picture they have drawn, watching them use a finger alphabet or waving a set of signal flags.

The good news: The human brain habituates patterns and symbols. For example, it converts the 26 letters of the alphabet into a code. Once the brain "breaks the code," the process of reading is possible. If the alphabet changes to a different language, then the brain must learn a new code.

The bad news: The human brain gets comfortable and even lazy when it habituates. It's stubborn. It likes to do things it already knows how to do. Learning new symbols and patterns can be tuff. It creates frustration and it takes practice.

More good news: Thinking exercises are good for the brain. The speed at which the brain processes information is increased when the brain learns to think in different ways, to decode new symbols and patterns. There is growing evidence that frequent stimulation of the brain using visual problem solving can help learning disabilities, improve over-all intelligence and even delay the effects of aging. In short, if you don't use it—you lose it!

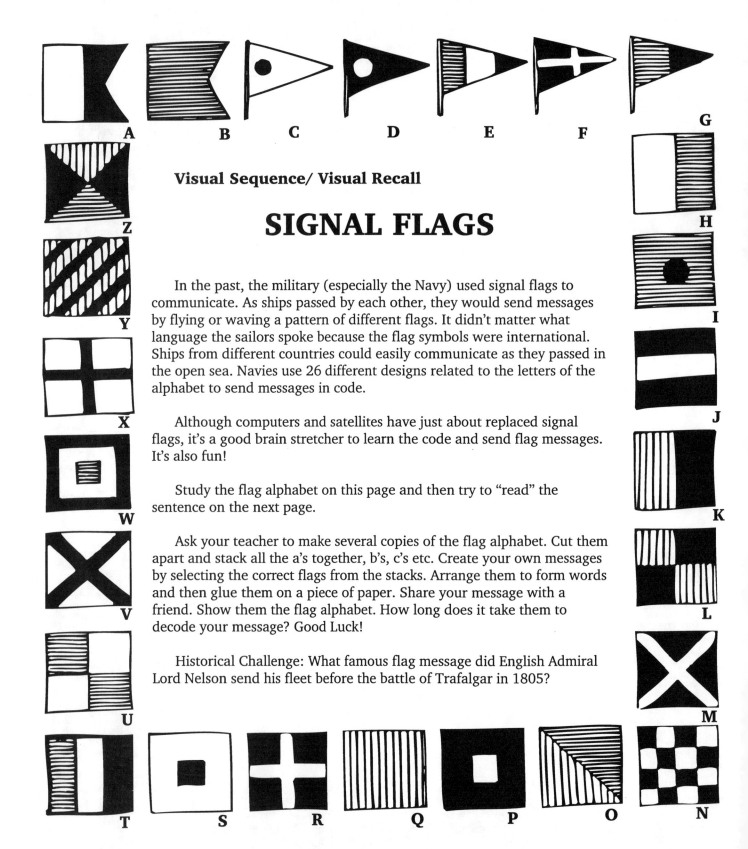

Visual Sequence/ Visual Recall

SIGNAL FLAGS

In the past, the military (especially the Navy) used signal flags to communicate. As ships passed by each other, they would send messages by flying or waving a pattern of different flags. It didn't matter what language the sailors spoke because the flag symbols were international. Ships from different countries could easily communicate as they passed in the open sea. Navies use 26 different designs related to the letters of the alphabet to send messages in code.

Although computers and satellites have just about replaced signal flags, it's a good brain stretcher to learn the code and send flag messages. It's also fun!

Study the flag alphabet on this page and then try to "read" the sentence on the next page.

Ask your teacher to make several copies of the flag alphabet. Cut them apart and stack all the a's together, b's, c's etc. Create your own messages by selecting the correct flags from the stacks. Arrange them to form words and then glue them on a piece of paper. Share your message with a friend. Show them the flag alphabet. How long does it take them to decode your message? Good Luck!

Historical Challenge: What famous flag message did English Admiral Lord Nelson send his fleet before the battle of Trafalgar in 1805?

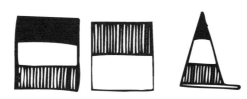

Look closer at the flags.
Can you decode the message?

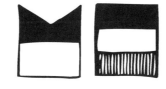

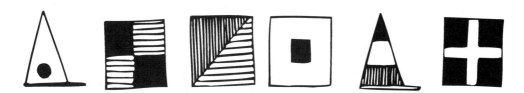

Message: _____

SIGN LANGUAGE

Sign language is a manual language of the deaf. It is a code in which the fingers and hands are used to illustrate the letters of the alphabet. The one-handed system is the most common. However, the deaf use a mixture of signs, gestures, facial expressions and lip-reading which in combination are as fast as normal speech. Sign language can also be an important visual thinking skill for those with hearing. It challenges the brain to communicate in new and different ways.

Memorizing the signs one at a time in isolation is difficult. Try signing the alphabet while singing the alphabet song. Practice signing a list of rhyming words where only the first letter in each word changes. (ham, Sam, ram, jam, etc.) Practice nursery rhymes or other familiar poems or songs. Learn the Pledge of Allegiance and say it every day. Practice! Practice!

SIGN LANGUAGE ALPHABET

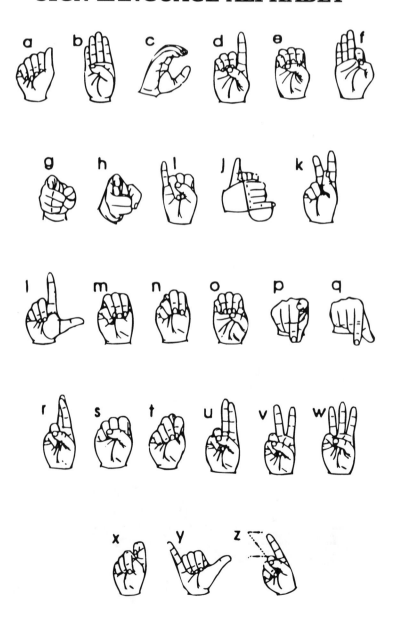

SIGN LANGUAGE

Look closer at the fingers. Can you decode the messages?

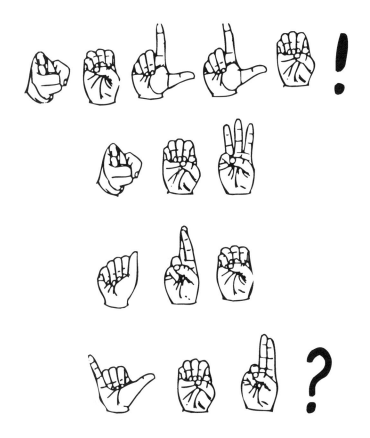

Message: _____?

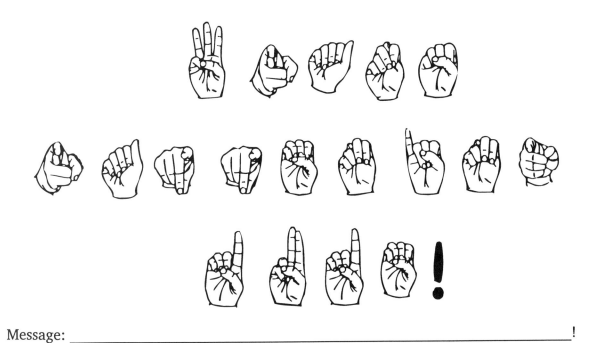

Message: _____!

Visual Synthesis/ Pattern Completion

This is a nursery rhyme. Can you recite it by "reading" the pictures?

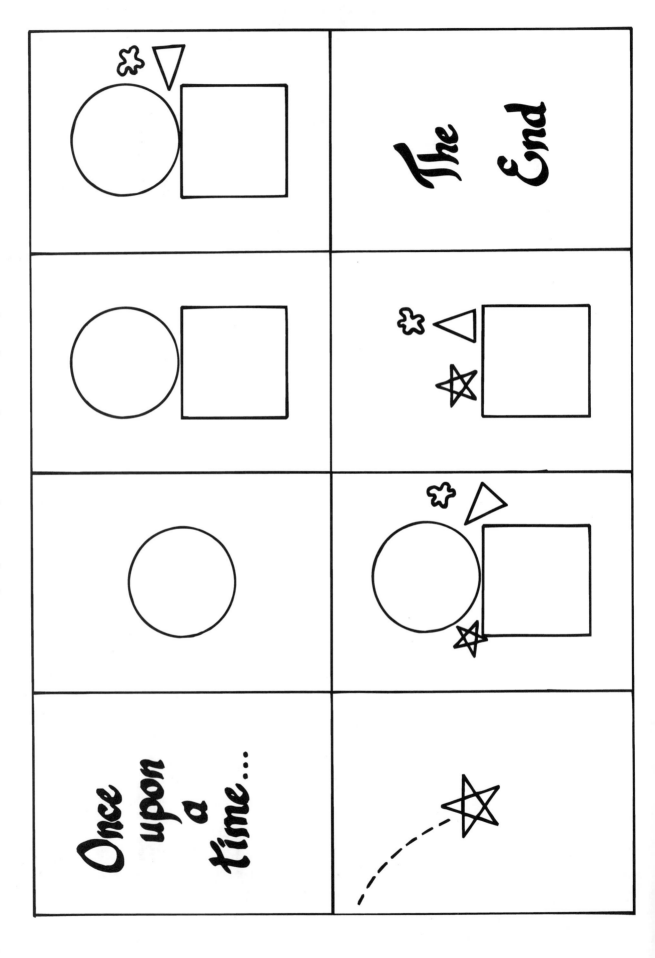

Visual Synthesis/ Pattern Completion

This is a nursery rhyme. Can you recite it by "reading" the pictures?

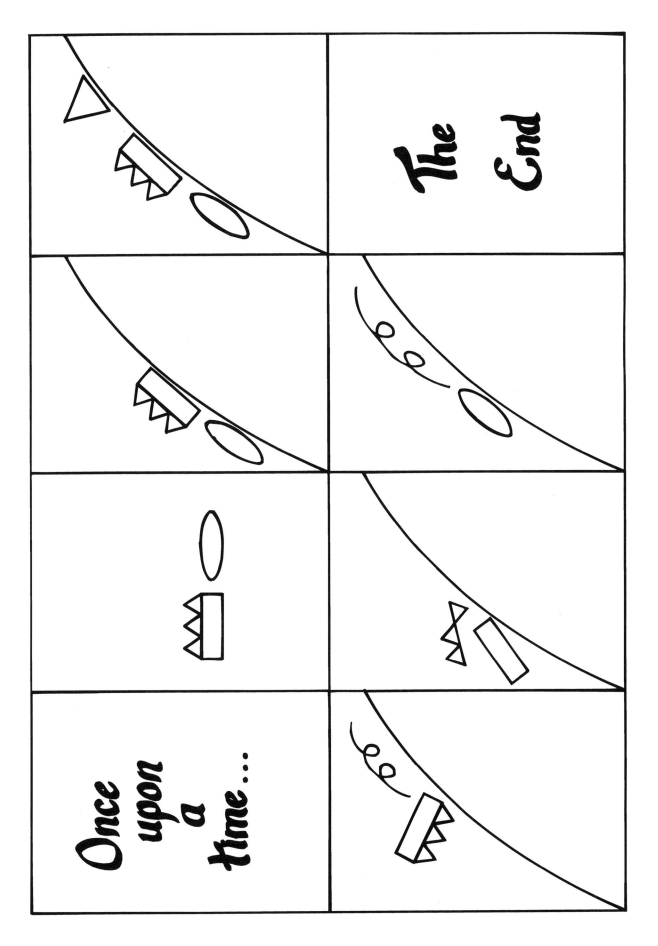

Choose a favorite nursery rhyme. Use symbols instead of words to tell the story.

			The End
Once upon a time...			

The Year In Pictures

Look at the facts about 1950. Then look at the picture symbols. Do they match? Research 1950. Try to add more information and more symbols. Could someone else guess the correct year just by looking at the symbols and not the words?

**LOOK CLOSER
AT
1950**

Who?

The President was Harry Truman.
The Vice President was Alben Barkley.
Natalie Cole and Tony Danza were born.
Nancy Johnson started first grade.

What?

Scientists discovered the structure of DNA.
Antihistamines were invented for stuffy noses.
The first nuclear submarine was launched.
Jerusalem became the capital of Israel.
Electric power from atomic energy was first used.
199,800 people attended a World Cup soccer tournament.

How Much?

The average family income was $3,200.
A gallon of milk cost $.80.
A new car cost $1,800.
A loaf of bread cost $.15.
A gallon of gas cost $.20.
A new house cost $15,000.
Nancy Johnson's father bought her a pony for $15.00.

Just For Fun

The favorite songs of most teenagers were *Mona Lisa* and *The Thing*.
The most popular movies were *All About Eve* and *Sunset Boulevard*.
Drive-in movies were the most popular attraction in the U.S.

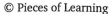

Fill the page with magazine pictures, newspaper clippings and drawings that symbolize 1960.

LOOK CLOSER
AT
1960

Who?
The President was Dwight Eisenhower.
The Vice President was Richard Nixon.
Ivan Lendl and Tracey Ullman were born.
Nancy Johnson was a sophomore in high school.

What?
The first weather satellite was sent into orbit.
Felt tip pens were invented.
The mini computer was patented.
Presidential debates were televised for the first time.
Olympics XVII were held in Italy.
Lasers were developed for commercial use.

How Much?
The average family income was $5,200.
A gallon of milk cost $1.00.
A new car cost $2,200.
A loaf of bread cost $.25.
A gallon of gas cost $.25.
A new house cost $30,000.

Just For Fun
Nancy Johnson and her friends were dancing The Twist.
The most popular songs were *Cathy's Clown* and *I'm Sorry*.
Spartacus, *Psycho* and *The Apartment* were popular movies.

Fill the page with magazine pictures, newspaper clippings and drawings that symbolize 1970.

LOOK CLOSER
AT
1970

Who?
The President was Richard Nixon.
The Vice President was Spiro Agnew.
Debbie Gibson, Mariah Carey and Ricky Shroder were born.
Nancy Johnson was teaching first grade in Moline, IL.

What?
Scientists completed the first synthesis of a gene.
Bar Codes were placed on products.
The floppy disk was invented.
The voting age was lowered to 18.
The first Earth Day was celebrated.
Apollo 13 was launched.
The number of U.S. troops in Vietnam was decreased.
Nancy Johnson missed three weeks of school because she had the mumps.

How Much?
The average family income was $9,500.
A gallon of milk was $1.30.
A new car cost $2,500.
A loaf of bread cost $.27.
A gallon of gas cost $.40.
A new house cost $40,000.

Just For Fun
People were humming along with *Close To You* and *Venus*.
John Wayne fans went to the movies to see *True Grit*.
Nancy Johnson made the last payment on her 1967 Mustang.

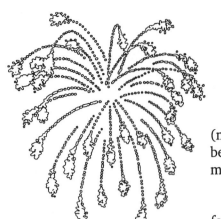

MARDI GRAS MASK

Mardi Gras is an exciting festival celebration. The word Mardi Gras (mar-dee-grah) means Fat Tuesday in French. It is the Tuesday before the beginning of the religious season known as Lent. Fat Tuesday ends a joyous month of parades, parties and carnivals.

Mardi Gras dates from the time when Christians had to use up all animal fat before Lent. The people would celebrate from January until the night before Ash Wednesday. Some Christians call the day before Lent begins Shrove Tuesday. "Shrove" is a word that means "to confess sins." On Shrove Tuesday people would go to church, confess their sins, and then go home for a big carnival.

French settlers brought the Mardi Gras festival to the United States. The states of Alabama, Florida, Louisiana, Mississippi, and Texas have annual Mardi Gras celebrations. The biggest and most famous Mardi Gras is in New Orleans, Louisiana. Many people with French ethnic background still live in Louisiana.

The citizens of New Orleans celebrate Mardi Gras with a carnival that lasts for ten days. People from all over the world come to New Orleans to join in the fun. They dress up in fancy costumes and masks and go to parties, balls and parades. The sponsors of most of the events are called Krewes. Each Krewe names a king and queen who ride on a special float in a parade. The royal couple tosses lagniappes to people watching the parade. Lagniappes (lan-yup) are free, un-asked-for gifts.

Mask Investigations

Knowledge: Define Mardi Gras, mask, costume, guise, make-up, lagniappe, masquerade and disguise.

Compile a Fact Sheet about celebrations, customs or occasions when people wear masks. Present your facts in the form of a MindMap.

Comprehension: Describe a mask you once wore at Halloween. Describe a time when you wanted to hide behind a mask because you were embarrassed.

Plan a trip to the Mardi Gras in New Orleans for your math class. Calculate the route, distance, method of travel and personal expenses.

Application: Research as many different kinds of masks as you can. Design, draw and construct a mask from paper plates, grocery bags, poster board and other materials.

Organize an art show/contest for the masks created by you and your friends. Create a "Judge's Worksheet" to be given to each person attending your "Gallery Of Masks." Collect the worksheets at the end of the show, analyze the data and present awards.

Analysis: Compare and contrast masks used in different celebrations or customs. (Mardi Gras, Halloween, Traditional African Tribal Ceremonies, Costume Ball, SCUBA Diving, Operating Room, Snow Skiing or Bank Robbery)

Compare and contrast the music that is heard when different masks are used for festivals, carnivals, holidays and other celebrations. Record examples and use them with your report.

Synthesis: Pretend you are Merlin The Magical Mask Maker and you have been hired to create a mask for a famous person. Write a story about your client and what happens when he/she discovers the new mask is magical.

Pretend you have just been selected as the king or queen of a Krewe parade. Write a diary describing the ten days of carnival before Fat Tuesday. Be sure to include information about all the parties, balls, parades and events that you reign over.

Design a line of greeting cards using your mask as the main design.

Compose a list of questions a Mardi Gras mask might ask a Ski mask. Include How come....?, What if....?, Point of View, Quantity and Compare/Contrast questions.

Evaluation: What if Halloween and Mardi Gras were suddenly declared illegal? Write a letter to a newspaper editor explaining your point of view.

What is your point of view about this statement?
"Everyone hides behind a mask at some time in their life."

MARDI GRAS MASK

Color the mask with the brightest, most colorful markers you can find. Add more decorations if you wish. (Glitter and ribbon would be great!)

MARDI GRAS MASK

Congratulations! You have just won the annual Mardi Gras Mask contest. Your unique design won first prize. Draw your design.

PICTURE THIS!

Arrange students in rows or lines. The first student in each of the rows studies the details in a picture. They are each looking at a copy of the same picture. The picture is returned to the teacher. The first student in each row then turns to the student immediately behind him/her and whispers a description of the picture.

The receiving student, who has not seen the picture, can ask as many questions as necessary to clarify or fill in the details of the mental picture being formed. When the receiving student in each row is satisfied with the picture in mind, he or she turns and describes the picture to the student immediately behind him or her.

After the last student in each row receives a description and asks questions to gain additional information, he/she draws a picture based on that mental image. The "winner" is the row whose picture is closest to the original drawing.

The teacher/facilitator should provide a fairly simple picture the first time. As students have more practice and increase their confidence, the level of difficulty can be increased. With a little practice, students will ask and answer better questions that result in more accurate information. Many students will challenge their teacher to find more difficult pictures with more finite details.

Picture This!

Picture This!

Picture This!

LOOK! - LISTEN! - DRAW!

This activity provides students with an excellent opportunity to sharpen listening skills using effective communication and **visual thinking**. During the activity they must ask questions that will explain information, formulate spatial relationships in their imagination, and then synthesize what they think they have heard. The result is improved memory abilities.

Organize students in triads. Two members sit with their backs to a screen. The third member faces the other two, able to see the screen; but the other two members cannot. Place a drawing on the overhead projector. The member who can see the screen has one minute to study the picture on the screen.

At the end of one minute, turn off the projector. Have the viewer describe the picture to the other members of the triad. Remind students since their partners cannot see what they are describing they must use lots of visual clues and details. The triad members who cannot see the screen may ask questions during the description to clarify the information they are receiving, but they may **not** take notes or draw. They must create a mental image of what they are hearing.

After one minute the triad member who has been describing **stops**, and the other two members draw the picture **from memory**. They must do this individually. Once they start drawing, students may not ask any questions or compare their drawings.

The follow-up/evaluation discussion involves comparing and contrasting the pictures drawn with the "real thing" on the screen.

Discuss the communication process.

Was there any information misunderstood or completely lost?

What other questions could have been asked to extract more details?

How did the time restriction affect the drawings?

All the describers were looking at the same image, but did they describe it in the same way?

All the drawers were drawing the same picture, but did each completed drawing look the same?

Practice makes perfect! The best activities are those the students want to do again and again. This activity fits the bill! By repeating the activity with other pictures, students will be surprised at the improvement in their listening and memory skills.

PICTURE PLAY

These 12 squares show what the Halloween picture looked like as the artist worked on it. Use your eyes to "play" with the pictures and put them in correct order. Number the pictures from 1-12.

PICTURE PLAY

Draw 12 different stages of the same picture. Number 12 will be the finished picture with the most details. Number 1 will be the first picture with the least details. When you have finished, cut the squares out. Ask a friend to put them in the correct sequence. Have fun!

1	**2**	**3**
4	**5**	**6**
7	**8**	**9**
10	**11**	**12**

WEATHER SYMBOLS

The National Weather Service uses over 100 visual symbols to explain
or forecast the weather. Study the following symbols. Practice drawing
each one on another piece of paper. Try to memorize them. Read the
weather map. Write a weather report on another piece of paper.

• rain   ≡ fog   ᔑ dust or sandstorm

△ hail   ᧁ drizzle   ℞ thunderstorm

✳ snow   ∞ haze   ﹏ cold front

▽ showers   ⌇⌇⌇ smoke   ﹏ warm front

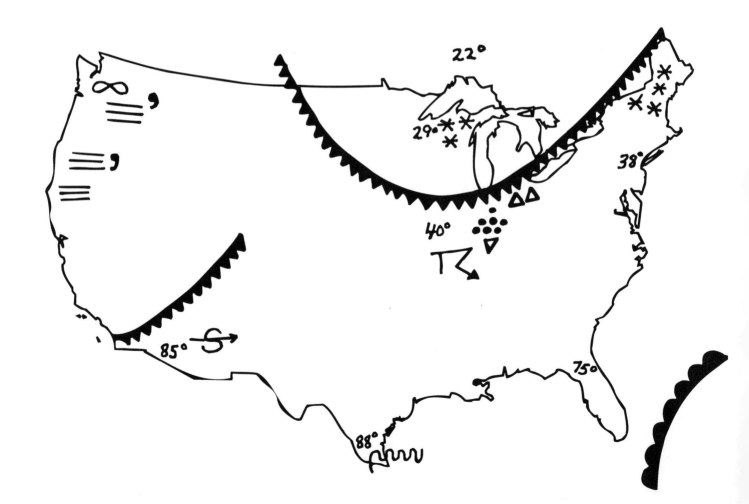

WEATHER SYMBOLS

Create two different weather maps using the symbols from the National Weather Service. Do a written report for each one.

THE CAT'S MEOW MAZE

How many different paths can your eyes follow from the cat's tail to his ears?

Start

LET ME OUTTA HERE!

Here is a super challenge maze. Using only your eyes (no finger pointing allowed) enter the maze wherever you wish. How long can your travel around inside the maze without going through an exit? Good Luck!

MR. DETAIL MAN

Elaboration is an important skill in visual thinking. Recognizing, adding, and remembering details are specific skills that can easily be improved. Some students may not have strong creative thinking abilities, i.e. "I can't think of nothin!" It is difficult for them to express their creativity if they can't even get started. However, if a base or starting point is provided, they can quickly add or elaborate on the idea.

Some students seem to have an innate sense of detail. Rebecca was the last student I put on the mural. When all the other "drawing committees" were finished with their portion of the mural, Rebecca would add details. From grass along the path, extra petals on flowers, eyelashes on people and animals, buttons on clothes, and knots on trees, to shadows, lines and squiggles Rebecca put her own personal touch on all our visual projects.

Once students learn to recognize and use visual details, the brain can easily apply that skill to reading and writing. Activities that stimulate visual detail make excellent readiness lessons for creative writing. The stories and poems that students write will suddenly be enriched with more descriptive language. Like magic, students seem to become more sensitive and aware of detail in their school assignments and in their lives.

Duplicate a copy of Mr. Detail Man for each student. Have students cut him out, glue him on a large piece of paper and draw a scene around him. Brainstorm a list of questions about Mr. Detail Man.

Where did Mr. Detail Man come from?
Where is he going?
Does Mr. Detail Man have a Detail Partner?
Does he have a Detail Car?
Does he have super powers? Why is he called Mr. Detail Man?
Is Mr. Detail Man on a secret mission?
What is his favorite thing to do?
Would Mr. Detail Man have a special Detail Diet?
What is his nickname?
What if Mr. Detail Man was in a movie or T.V. show?
What worries Mr. Detail Man?
How is he like a real human being? How is he different?

The answers to the questions should be found in the pictures that students draw in the scene. Encourage students to "saturate" their drawings with DETAILS!

Follow Up: Students can write a story, poem, play, book, song or rap about the scene they drew. They can pretend to be a newspaper reporter and interview Mr. Detail Man for a feature article. They can pretend to be Mr. Detail Man and write a letter of advice to all the kids in North America.

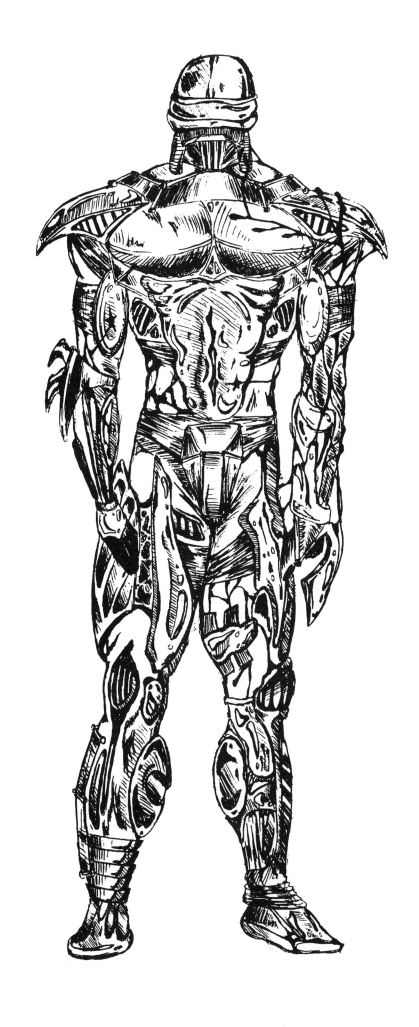

SAY CHEESE!

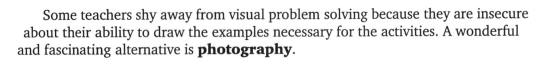

Some teachers shy away from visual problem solving because they are insecure about their ability to draw the examples necessary for the activities. A wonderful and fascinating alternative is **photography**.

Teachers and students can use the simplest, most inexpensive camera equipment to begin their journey into the world of visual thinking. They will quickly learn the rules of the craft, yet maintain the freedom and individuality of choosing their own subject material.

Stan and Kathy Balsamo have developed (excuse the pun!) their skills of photography far beyond the Instamatic stage. However, they will be the first to tell you they are still learning. The examples on page 104 of their work are meant to motivate personal explorations by teachers and students.

"Photography can be as universal as the musical world to young and old. Although color photography is breathtaking, more possibilities exist for the imagination with black and white photography, much like radio stimulated the imagination while television stunted it."

"Combining photography and visual problem solving activities gives excellent opportunities for all ages to use the skills of analysis, synthesis and evaluation while drawing upon knowledge and application. It also utilizes the creativity components of fluency, flexibility, elaboration, and originality as well as exercising both hemispheres of the brain."——*"A Closer Look"* by Stan and Kathy Balsamo. CHALLENGE Magazine, 1983, Good Apple Inc.

Questions and Ideas

How many different things could this be? (Be sure to look at each photo from ALL angles and viewpoints.

List every possible characteristic and detail in each photo. Ask a friend to do the same. Compare and contrast your lists.

Choose one photo. What are all the things it COULDN'T be?

Which photo is your personal favorite? Why? Which photo would you hate to see as a wallpaper pattern in your room? Why?

Transform one photo into a fabric design by repeating it several times on a separate piece of paper. Draw an article of clothing or a piece of furniture using your design.

How many different colors could the design in the photo be? Would changing the color change what it is, its usefulness?

Choose two photos. Compare and contrast them.

Choose one part or detail from a photo. Expand it. Extend it into something else. Change it in some way. Make it bigger or smaller. Repeat it. Add new details from another photo. What has happened to your original design? Put it somewhere else and give it a new function.

"Improve" one photo by adding color or texture such as yarn, cloth, or other collage materials.

Pretend a photo is part of something else. Glue the photo to the middle of a large piece of drawing paper. Complete the photo by drawing the entire object around the photo.

Experiment with computer graphics. How many of the photo designs can you copy or replicate on the computer?

Categorize the photos in as many ways as possible.

Which photo stimulates the most emotion in you or your friends? Describe how you feel when you look at each photo. Does the picture remind you of something funny or scary?

Create a new invention using one or more of the photos.

Draw your favorite sports car. Use the designs in the photos to create a new paint job.

Compose a list of your own questions using these photographs and designs.

Go out at take your own pictures and then compose another list of questions.

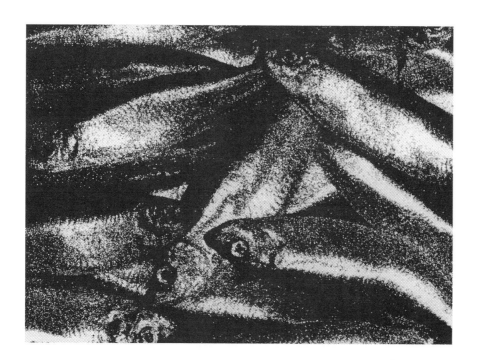

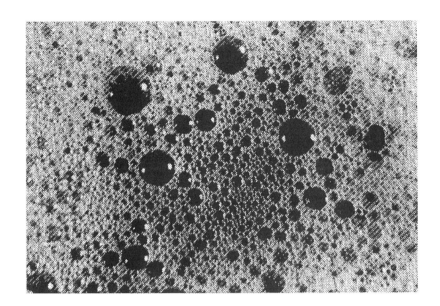

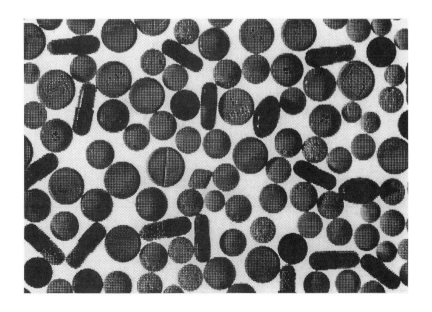

VISUAL THINKING WITH COLOR

Motivation is the primary concern of most teachers. Providing stimulating, differentiated curriculum to an unmotivated student is at the most a waste of time and at the least frustrating. Sometimes a new teaching technique combined with a better understanding of brain function and learning styles can make all the difference.

Emotion is the key to motivation. One of the most powerful ways to stimulate emotion is through the use of color. In his book, **Color In Your Life** (New York: The John Day Company, 1962) Irving Adler describes the use of color and its ability to stimulate or calm human emotions.

Because people see colors with their hearts, not just their eyes, they have the power to change moods. Teachers can harness the mood-making energies of color in their classrooms. Color can invigorate or tranquilize, stimulate language development or put students to sleep.

Most people respond to the effects of color in similar ways. Yellow, orange, lime green and red are activating colors. They are the extroverts of the rainbow. They expand, warm, cheer and communicate. Most important, they increase the energy in the people they surround.

Corals, peaches and ambers are stimulating to appetites while blues, dark greens and purples are restful and calming. The neutral colors or "uncolors" of the rainbow are beige, browns, taupe, and gray. They neither activate or pacify; they just blend. The knowledge and understanding of the effects of color is important for those teaching LD, BD, ADD and ADHD students. A case in point:

Connie had taught first grade for 20 years but could never remember a student as challenging as Nathan. His attention span was short, his ability to focus was obviously impaired, and he never stopped moving. She worried every day about his chances of advancing to second grade. She was desperate for ideas that might help him.

Connie began to experiment with color and its effect on Nathan. She covered the top of Nathan's desk with a large piece of colored construction paper. It served as a mat for him to work on. No matter how many books or worksheets Nathan stacked on his desk, there were always small sections of the colored mat visible around the edges.

Like magic, Connie began to notice a change in Nathan's work habits. It all depended on what color the mat was. On the day bright yellow was used, he didn't hand in a single finished paper. On the day a medium blue was used, Connie found two completed worksheets in her basket. Color didn't solve all of Nathan's problems, but you will never convince Connie that color didn't play a major role in getting him into second grade!

LOOK CLOSER AT YOU!

Face Paint

Recipe:

1 Teaspoon Moisturizer
1 Teaspoon Cold Cream
4 to 5 Teaspoons Corn Starch
1/2 Teaspoon Water
Drops of Food Coloring

Start with moisturizer, cold cream and corn starch. Adjust water and corn starch to get the right consistency. Egg cartons make great paint holders. Provide several brushes, various sizes and shapes. Have paper towels and extra cold cream handy to wipe off mistakes!

Encourage students to think through a design before they attack a real face! Provide paper and colored pens for practice. The designs may or may not have a theme (holidays, symbols, seasons, plants, environment, cartoons, animals, people, etc.) The face painting can be part of a book report presentation, art lesson, science project, thematic unit or literature appreciation.

Take photographs of the finished product for a group scrapbook.

Face painting can be pure fun, but it also has a serious side. It is one of the oldest human art forms. From cavemen in Europe to tribal chiefs in Africa; from Native Americans in South Dakota to Clowns in Sarasota, Florida, face painting has important significance, power and symbolism. A discussion and/or research project about the history of face painting will help students understand and appreciate different cultures and customs.

THE BUGS ARE COMING!
THE BUGS ARE COMING!

Fill up this page with many **different** drawings of insects and bugs. They can be imaginary. Create your own design for a 25th Century Bug.

THE DINOSAUR DREAM

Add more details to the border and write a story in the middle.

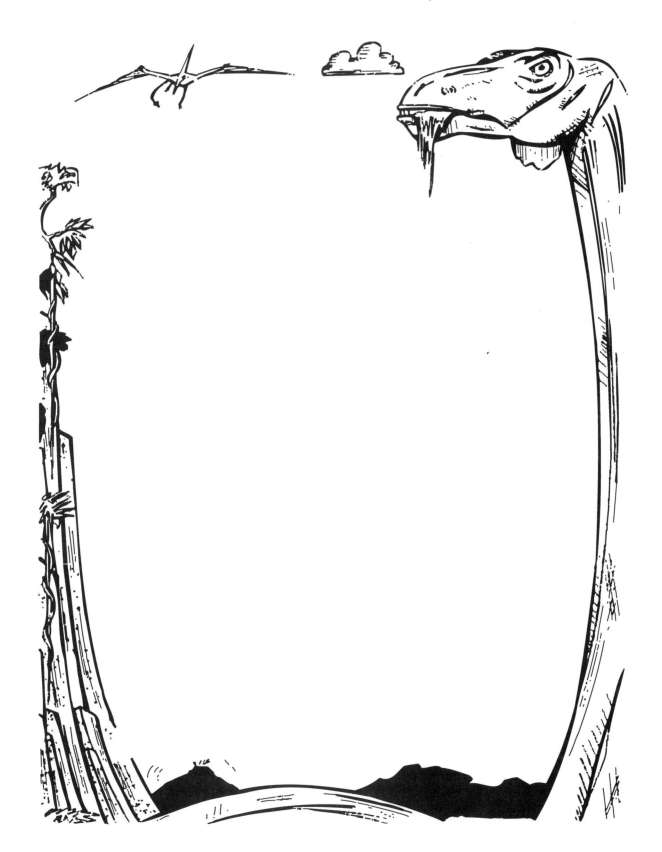

SEE - RUN - DO POSTERS

Once in a great while an activity comes along that combines several kinds of thinking and stimulates several learning styles. See-Run-Do posters require the integration of visual/kinesthetic thinking with strong communication skills. It is a flexible activity that can easily be adapted to fit different grade levels or subject areas. Best of all, it's lots of fun! It will become a student favorite.

The object of the activity is for each group to construct a poster that looks like the sample poster.

Teacher Pre-activity: Construct a sample See-Run-Do poster to use during the group activity. Do NOT let students see the poster.

Materials Needed: markers, scissors, glue, tape, construction paper, newspaper, yarn and various collage materials.

Construction By Teacher: Use standard size white poster board. The sample poster might have a theme such as a season, holiday, famous person or event. Or construct a poster that is not limited to one theme. The pictured poster has a rainforest theme.

Procedure: Draw two-dimensional shapes, symbols or animals on the poster board. Glue a three-dimensional shape such as a cylinder, tube or cone on the poster. Cut newspaper into silhouette shapes representing clouds, buildings or vines. Glue them to the poster. Glue other collage materials to the poster (feathers, pipe cleaners, crepe paper, pasta, etc.)

Student Activity: Assign students to groups of six or seven. Ask each group to select two VERY VERBAL people. (Teacher may choose to do this.) One will be the DESCRIBER. The other will be the RUNNER. The rest of the students will be poster makers.

Provide materials for other group members to choose from. Include the same materials the teacher used to construct the sample poster.

The Describer: Hang the sample poster outside the classroom. Describers remain outside the classroom during the entire activity. Only the describers may look at the sample poster. NO ONE ELSE SEES IT UNTIL THE ACTIVITY IS COMPLETELY OVER! After a describer looks at the sample poster, he moves away from the poster to a pre-determined spot also outside the classroom to talk to his runner. He describes the poster to the runner, a few details at a time. The runner runs back into the classroom with the information from the describer. While the runner is gone, the describers may look at the poster again. The describers may look at the sample poster as many times as they want. At no time, may the describers go back into the classroom and look at their groups' interpretation of the description. They get to see the group's poster after the time limit for the activity has expired.

The Runner: The runner returns to the classroom and communicates the describer's description of the poster to his/her group. Because he did not see the sample poster, he must rely on his visual memory and his describer to give him the details he needs to relay an accurate description to the group. The runner may make as many trips as he wishes between the group and the describer. The runner may NOT touch any group materials or use his hands when he returns to talk to his group. Each group of poster makers may ask their runner as many questions as they want.

A time limit of 20 to 30 minutes, depending on the complexity of the sample poster, guarantees the describers and runners make every minute count!

Follow Up: After the time limit expires, gather all the describers, runners, and poster makers together. Compare/contrast the posters from each group with the sample poster. Process the entire activity by asking the students to reflect on their feelings about it. Questions to consider: How did the runners communicate without using their hands? Was it easier being a describer, runner, or poster maker? How did the time limit affect the activity?

THE BOX

"I found it on the porch,
Sitting by itself.
A great big box with lots of locks,
Addressed to me, myself."

"That box is making noises,
As it sits there all alone.
It wiggles and it jiggles,
I think I hear it moan."

   Use the lines and illustrations from the Joe Wayman poem, THE BOX, to shake up your imagination. What do you think is in the box? Who sent it to you? Why? Is it something real or imaginary? What will happen when you open it? Draw a picture of what comes out and then write a story, poem or play about The Box.

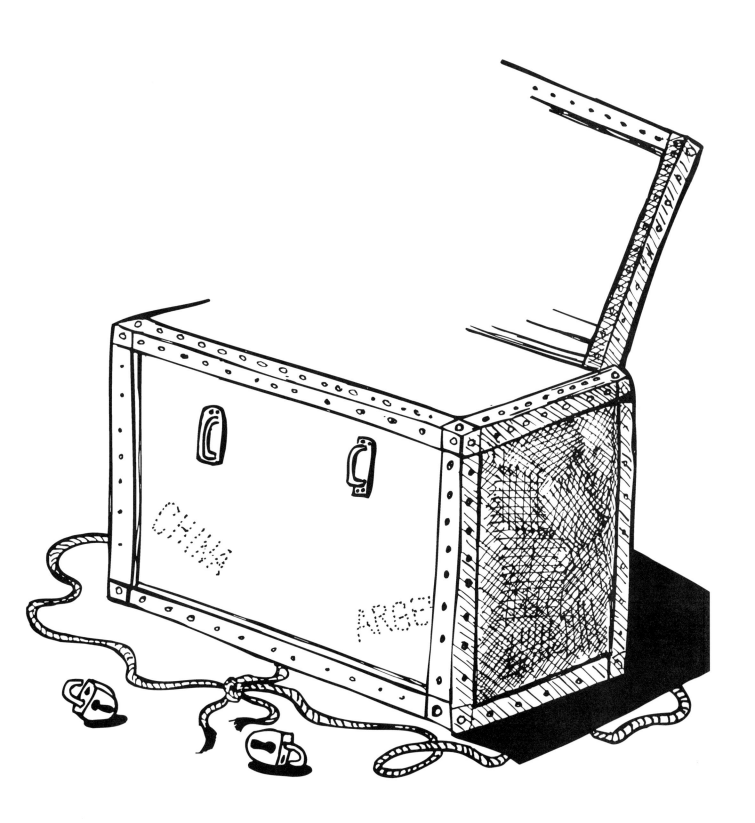

DESIGN COMPLETION

Completed Design

How did the artist complete this design? Number the steps from 1 to 5.

_____

_____

_____

_____

_____

114

FIESTA!

Complete the pattern by drawing the next correct illustration in the border.
Then write a story inside the border that includes the illustrations.

LET IT SNOW!

Find the two snowflakes that are alike.

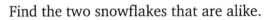

MUSEUM DETECTIVE

Original

5 artists were asked to duplicate a Zuni Indian sand painting. Only 1 artist completed it correctly. Check the painting done correctly. Circle the mistakes on the other 4 works.

_____

_____

_____

MIRROR DRAWING

Can you complete the other side of this symmetrical drawing?

MORE MIRROR DRAWING

Can you complete the other side of this symmetrical drawing?

Bill Jensen

IN YOUR MIND'S EYE

cat *(kat) noun, a carnivorous mammal of the family Felidae, including the domestic cat Felis catus. There are over 30 species in the cat clan, from 800-pound tigers to a tiny Asian cat that only weighs three pounds. Cats are native to all countries except Australia and Antarctica. They have super nocturnal vision, better than humans. Their eyes are six times more sensitive to the blue end of the light spectrum. They also have acute hearing and a well-developed sense of equilibrium. We humans have loved and nurtured cats since the Egyptians domesticated them before 3000 BC.*

Use Bill Jensen's beautiful cat illustration as a symbol or mascot in your classroom for visual thinking.

Duplicate a copy for each student as a cover for a special portfolio or scrapbook on visual thinking.

MORE MIRROR DRAWING

Can you complete the other side of this symmetrical drawing?

Postscript

There is fascinating and exciting new information being published every day about learning and brain function. A recent headline from *MONITOR*, The American Psychological Association Journal reads: *"Spatial reasoning may be music to a child's ears."*

New research released at a recent American Psychological Association convention confirms an earlier finding that musical activity enhances human spatial reasoning. It doesn't seem to matter whether the activity is taking music lessons or simply listening to music. The results are powerful.

The research was presented in a paper *"Music and spatial task performance: a causal relationship."* The research was conducted by Dr. Frances H. Rauscher, Dr. Gordon L. Shaw, Dr. Linda J. Levine and Katherine N. Ky of the University of California, Irvine; and Eric L. Wright of the Irvine Conservatory of Music.

The most important results from their study consist of the following points:

1. Listening to 10 minutes of Mozart's *Piano Sonata K 448* over a period of time before solving visual puzzles increased spatial IQ scores in college students. It only worked with Mozart's music. Other styles of music did not produce the same results.

2. The spatial reasoning skills of 19 preschool children who were given eight months of music lessons far exceeded the spatial reasoning performance of 15 children who had no musical training.

3. Music can improve intelligence for long periods of time, maybe even permanently.

4. It is important to involve children in music—the more the better.

5. Children who'd had musical training scored an average 14.0 on object-assembly tasks, while those with no training scored an average 10.4.

6. School administrators need to hear the message that musical training may help students' school performance.

7. Music education may be a valuable tool for the enhancement of preschool children's intellectual development.

Teachers and parents should take notice of this terrific good news. Why not experiment with a little Mozart before doing some of the activities in this book?

Bibliography

Aust, Siegfried, LENSES! TAKE A CLOSER LOOK. Lerner Publications, 1991.

Balsamo, Kathy, IT'S ABOUT WRITING. Beavercreek, OH.: Pieces of Learning, 1990.

Balsamo, Kathy, THEMATIC ACTIVITIES FOR STUDENT PORTFOLIOS. Beavercreek, OH.: Pieces of Learning, 1994.

de Bono, Tony, THINK. New York: Basic Books, 1968.

de Mille, Robert, PUT YOUR MOTHER ON THE CEILING. New York: Walker & Co., 1967.

GAMES Magazine. Workman Publishing Co., 708 Broadway, New York, N.Y. 10003.

Gordon, W.J.J., SYNECTICS. New York: Harper & Row, 1961.

Gregory, R.L., EYE AND BRAIN. New York: McGraw/Hill Paperbacks, 1966.

Huxley, A., THE ART OF SEEING. New York: Harper & Row, 1942.

Johnson, Nancy, THINKING IS THE KEY. Beavercreek, Oh.: Pieces of Learning, 1993.

Johnson, Nancy, THE BEST TEACHER STUFF. Beavercreek, Oh.: Pieces of Learning, 1994.

Johnson, Nancy, ACTIVE QUESTIONING. Beavercreek, Oh.: Pieces of Learning, 1995.

Macaulay, David, THE WAY THINGS WORK. Boston: Houghton Mifflin, 1988.

McKim, Robert H., THINKING VISUALLY. Palo Alto, CA.: Dale Seymour, 1980.

MAZE 'til ya CRAZE. A set of 4 different mazes. Compoz-A-Puzzle, One Robert Lane, Glen Head, NY 11545

Paraguin, Charles Heinz, THE WORLD'S BEST OPTICAL ILLUSTIONS. Sterling Publishing, 1987.

PUZZLEGRAMS, A Fireside Book. New York: Simon & Schuster, 1989.

Rubin, Don, BRAINSTORMS. New York: Harper Row, 1988.

Simon, Seymour, THE OPTICAL ILLUSION BOOK. Four Winds Press, 1976.

Wayman, Joseph, THE OTHER SIDE OF READING. Carthage, IL.: Good Apple Inc., 1980.

Solutions & Answers

Page 13
the one on the right

Page 30
1 yes
2 neither
3 straight
4 no

Page 31
yes-yes-no
both-vase and two profiles

Page 32
neither-black-black
black-black-black
D-B-E-A-C

Page 34
1-H	2-I	3-C	4-E	5-J
6-A	7-B	8-D	9-F	10-G

Page 36
( ) (X)   ( )
( ) (X)   ( )   ( )
( ) ( )   ( )   (X)
( ) ( )   (X)   ( )

Page 37
( ) ( )   (X)
( ) (X)   ( )
( ) (X)   ( )

Page 38
( ) (X)   ( )
( ) (X)   ( )   ( )
( ) ( )   ( )   (X)
(X) ( )   ( )   ( )

Page 44
HELLO
SLIME
ZERO
QUACK
GREEN
JUMP

Page 46
circle opposite smile
ice cream opposite flower
star opposite heart
smile opposite circle
flower opposite ice cream
heart opposite star

Page 48
( ) (X)   ( )
( ) ( )   (X)
( ) (X)   ( )

Page 62

Page 63

Page 64
B, H

Page 65
F, H

Page 66
No, No
No, Yes

Page 68
8E, 4B, 6G, 2D, 5D
7D, 11F, 3E, 2F, 9B

Page 71

126

Page 72
19 solid black gum balls—don't forget the one in the base!
200 total gum balls

Page 73
77 flies

Page 76
Admiral Lord Nelson'smessage:
"England expects that every man will do his duty."

Page 77
Look closer at all the different flags

Page 79
Hello! How are you?
What's happening dude!

Page 80
Little Miss Muffet/Sat on a tuffet/Eating her curds and whey/
Along came a spider/And sat down beside her/And frightened Miss Muffet away.

Page 81
Jack and Jill/Went up the hill/To fetch a pail of water/
Jack fell down/And broke his crown/And Jill came tumbling after

Page 94

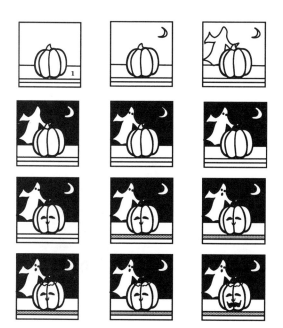

Page 114
1,4
5,3, 2

Page 115

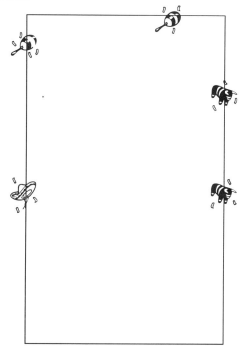

Page 116

Page 177
top left sand painting is correct
top right - missing ears
middle - missing 1 line in banner
bottom left added neckline
bottom right colored 2 black tail feathers

Nancy Johnson's Workshops are DYNAMIC!

Invite Nancy Johnson to your
School
School district
Inservice day
Parent Meeting
Teacher Institute
Educational Service Center
State & Regional Conference

for the most dynamic, practical, and fun
presentation you've ever experienced!

"I came to get my "fix" of Nancy. I can never get enough of her!"
"Thank you! When I get back Monday, I'll awaken brain cells and
you'll hear the excitement from wherever you are. My brain is
popping with ideas. Thanks so much for getting it going."
"We appreciate the timely messages, the enthusiasm and
excitement which you instilled in all of us. You are one special lady."

Teachers & Administrators say . . .

Sampling of Topics

Questioning & Thinking Skills
Gifted Education
Creative Activities for All Classrooms
Global Education
Differentiating Curriculum
Visual Thinking Skills for All Students
Favorite Keynote -
  The Teacher Makes the Difference

Author of

Active Questioning
The BEST Teacher 'Stuff'
The Faces of Gifted
Thinking is the Key
Questioning Makes the Difference
and videos . . .
Teaching Skills for the 90's
Parenting Skills for the 90's

Catch the Enthusiasm! Schedule Nancy for inservice.   Call Pieces of Learning! 1-800-729-5137